Haunted
Places
of
Warwickshire

Rupert Matthews

COUNTRYSIDE BOOKS
NEWBURY, BERKSHIRE

First published 2005
© Rupert Matthews 2005

COUNTRYSIDE BOOKS
3 Catherine Road
Newbury, Berkshire

To view our complete range of books,
please visit us at
www.countrysidebooks.co.uk

ISBN 1 85306 925 6
EAN 9781 85306 925 3

Cover picture from an original
painting by Anthony Wallis

Photographs by the author

Designed by Peter Davies, Nautilus Design
Produced through MRM Associates Ltd., Reading
Typeset by Jean Cussons Typesetting, Diss, Norfolk
Printed by Arrowsmith, Bristol

•Contents•

The **Haunted** places of **Warwickshire**

NOTE: THIS MAP IS NOT TO SCALE

LEICESTERSHIRE

Watling Street

Fosse Way

POLESWORTH

BIRMINGHAM

OLDBURY

HARTSHILL

ASTLEY

WOLVEY

COOMBE ABBEY

COVENTRY

CANLEY

BRANDON

BAGINTON

KENILWORTH

LITTLE LAWFORD

RUGBY

River Avon

BADDESLEY CLINTON

GUYS CLIFFE

PRINCETHORPE

WOOTTON WAWEN

WARWICK

ROYAL LEAMINGTON SPA

STUDLEY

WARWICKSHIRE

SHUCKBURGH

COUGHTON COURT

NAPTON ON THE HILL

WORCESTERSHIRE

ALCESTER

STRATFORD UPON AVON

HARBURY

RAGLEY HALL

RED HILL

CHARLECOTE PARK

LIGHTHORNE

River Avon

ATHERSTONE ON STOUR

BURTON DASSETT

NORTHAMPTONSHIRE

PRESTON ON STOUR

EDGEHILL

MEON HILL

ILMINGTON

HONINGTON

BRAILES

OXFORDSHIRE

LONG COMPTON

LITTLE COMPTON

GLOUCESTERSHIRE

HAUNTED PLACE

COUNTY BOUNDARY

• Introduction •

Without doubt Warwickshire is one of the most scenic of English counties. There are hills, cliffs, valleys and broad plains. And there are the ghosts, of course. Before I began the enjoyable task of travelling Warwickshire to research this book, I knew about a few of the phantoms that lurk in this charming county, but I was entirely unprepared for the sheer number and variety of ghosts that I would uncover as I went. The rich, famous and powerful crowd together in the phantom scene of Warwickshire, with royalty, nobility and religious leaders all to be found in spectral form across the county.

By no means, though, are all the ghosts of Warwickshire of famous or historic personages. A great many of the more startling apparitions are of local folk of no great fame or notoriety. The ghost lorry of the main road east of Coventry careers along the highway with lights blazing, a reminder of a horrific traffic accident some years ago. Other spectres are even more anonymous. The Stag pub at Red Hill has a lady phantom that is among the most active in the country – though also one of the least frightening.

Of course, some people will insist that there are no such things as ghosts. Well, they are entitled to their views. Having travelled back and forth across Warwickshire to track down the spectral inhabitants of the county, I can confirm that there are hundreds of sober, respectable folk who have seen ghosts and phantoms. Let the sceptics explain that, if they will. In any case, sceptics are very often simply those who have not yet seen a ghost for themselves.

I have enjoyed my time in Warwickshire, visiting pubs and stately homes, village streets and remote stretches of highway. And, as this book shows, I have been able to uncover a most amazingly varied and active collection of ghosts and spectres. It remains only for you to get out there and enjoy this lovely area of England for yourself. Just watch out for the ghosts.

Rupert Matthews

•North Warwickshire•

POLESWORTH

I
f you are looking for history, tradition and ghosts then this is the place to visit. Today a rather rambling settlement that is a cross between a town and a village, it was once the bustling centre of northern Warwickshire.

Polesworth's rise to prosperity began in AD 825 on the bloodstained battlefield of Ellendun, many miles to the south in Wiltshire. Warwickshire was then the heart of the kingdom of Mercia, a powerful English state that imposed an overlordship over several neighbouring kingdoms. The kingdom of Wessex, stretching from Devon to Sussex, was not one to acknowledge Mercian rule. When King Ceolwulf of Mercia was deposed for incompetence and replaced by an obscure nobleman named Beornwulf, King Egbert of Wessex took advantage to seize disputed borderlands in Wiltshire. This led to the Battle of Ellendun, at which the Mercians were comprehensively defeated.

Egbert of Wessex moved quickly to reach deals with the Kings of Sussex, Kent and East Anglia before moving into Mercia to establish himself as the new ruler there. But the victory did far more for Egbert than give him command over most of the English nation. It also solved a tricky family dispute.

Egbert had various children, but it was a daughter named Edith who was the problem. She was well educated and had taken a strong inclination to the religious life. Indeed, her knowledge of scripture and yearning for good morals were well known at Egbert's court. Rather too well known for some. She was forever reminding the nobles and warriors about the sin of gluttony, just as they were about to tuck into a feast, banging on about vanity to a lady who had acquired a new dress or talking at length about sloth when somebody was late for an appointment. By AD 830 something had to be done.

Fortunately there were extensive landholdings in Mercia whose owners had been killed at Ellendun. Among these was the little village of Polesworth. Egbert gave the village and its surrounding lands to his saintly daughter Edith and told her to go there, found a nunnery and do God's work. Edith was delighted. Pausing only long enough to remind her father that she would need ready cash to build the religious house, she travelled north to take up her new role. There she founded a convent, which she filled with the daughters of gentry who preferred a religious life, and settled down to the work of running a strict house.

In time, Edith passed away. She was buried in her beloved church at Polesworth. Before long, miracles began to occur at her tomb and she was formally recognised as a saint. The nuns of Polesworth continued to lead blamelessly holy lives, industriously working their lands and supervising their peasants to make a profit and do God's work. Even when Viking war-bands roamed the countryside, the Polesworth nuns went on with their duties.

Then came the Norman Conquest of 1066. William the Conqueror, now King William I of England, seized the holdings of English nobles and parcelled them out to his own supporters in thanks for their help in battle. Sir Robert Marmion got extensive lands in northern Warwickshire, which carried with them the duty of providing military protection and law courts for Polesworth and area. Arriving at Tamworth Castle to survey his new property, Sir Robert decided that if he were going to spend money protecting Polesworth, he might as well get some profit from the deal. He rode over with a gang of armed men and threw the nuns out while he pillaged the convent treasury and took ownership of the lands. The nuns retired to a small outlying cell they owned at Oldbury and sent messages to the King begging for the return of what was rightfully theirs.

As it turned out they did not need to wait for royal justice, divine justice was on its way.

Sir Robert rode back to Tamworth and organised a great feast to celebrate his acquisitions. St Edith must have disapproved very strongly of her convent property being put to such sinful use. That very night, as Sir Robert was getting ready for bed, her ghost appeared to him in his private chamber. She demanded he return her lands to her convent and struck Sir Robert on the ribs with her crozier, whereupon he collapsed in agony, his entire right side paralysed. Next morning Sir Robert's servants carried him to Tamworth church where he took solemn vows to return the stolen lands to Polesworth Convent. Slowly his health recovered and by the time the nuns had repaired their church and buildings he was well enough to take to the saddle.

Through the centuries that followed, the convent at Polesworth flourished. The village high street became the site for the Mop Fair at which agricultural labourers from across northern Warwickshire came on the first Saturday of October to find work for the coming year. Markets were established, ensuring that the little town was the economic heart of the rich surrounding farmland.

The old gatehouse at Polesworth, a solid reminder of the convent that once dominated the town.

Then came the Reformation of the reign of King Henry VIII in the 1540s. The King sent his commissioners and soldiers to Polesworth to close down the convent and seize its assets, just as all other religious houses were being closed down across England. It was time for St Edith to return, and so she did. But by this time her power must have been diminished somewhat. Rather than strike the King, she merely began walking the grounds of her convent. This gave the soldiers a bit of a fright, but did nothing to stop their work. Within months the lands and buildings had been sold off to the highest bidder. The church was put to use serving the parishioners of Polesworth and the gatehouse made into a private residence, but most of the

An old doorway that dates back to medieval times in the churchyard at Polesworth. The ghostly nun wanders the site of the old convent.

buildings were torn down and their materials used to build houses more suited to the local folk. The site of the cloisters and refectory became an open field beside the church.

And St Edith walks here still. She is seen several times each year, pacing sadly across the empty field, past the church and on towards the gatehouse. She no longer seeks to impose punishment on those who occupy church lands or live in houses built with stones from her convent. Instead she seems content merely to walk about her old property, perhaps seeking still to remind her fellow humans of their sinful condition.

OLDBURY

The village of Oldbury is really little more than a hamlet, with a scattering of houses along the twisting lane from Bentley to Hartshill. There is simply not a large enough population to maintain the shops and services of other, larger villages. The old Blue Bell Inn, for instance, is now a private house.

This has not put off the slightly sozzled old ghost who began his hauntings of the lane when the pub was still a pub, about a hundred years ago. The man in question was a servant named William Parker who worked at Brades Hall. The village hostelry at Oldbury was close enough for Parker to reach with ease, but far enough away that he would be out of sight of his employers. There he could relax and indulge his taste for fine beer before wending his way home.

The ghost at Oldbury is rather the worse for drink.

One unfortunate evening a storm blew up while Parker was cosily ensconced in the pub. By the time he got up to leave, heavy rain was sleeting over the Warwickshire hills. Parker huddled against the wall for shelter as a particularly fierce blast of wind hit the building. Sadly for Parker, the chimney high above him toppled over and crashed down, killing him instantly.

Ever since, the ghost of unfortunate William Parker has been seen late in the evening staggering along the lane, seemingly fighting to make headway against a ferocious wind. Even if the weather is quite calm, the coat of the ghost flaps as if buffeted by a howling gale.

HARTSHILL

The ghost of Hartshill is unidentified, but nobody is in any doubt that she is best avoided. Bad luck seems to dog those who attract her attention, though those who are passed by tend to escape without mishap.

The phantom lady is seen moving slowly about the ruins of Hartshill Castle, which dominate the northern end of the village. The castle was first built in the immediate wake of the Norman Conquest in the 1060s, when the Normans threw up fortified posts to overawe the English. The earthworks date from this period, with their 18 foot deep trenches and towering mounds. Hartshill Castle was never large, but it was secure enough to act as the headquarters of Henry Tudor, soon to be King Henry VII, before the Battle of Bosworth at which he won the crown.

The ghost that walks through the ruins of Hartshill Castle brings bad luck in its wake.

The stone walls that once topped these fortifications were torn down in the 1560s and replaced by a comfortable Tudor mansion. It is this building that is gently falling into ruin, and to which the ghost seems to belong. Her long silk dress and angular headdress point to an Elizabethan date.

One witness who encountered the ghost as he walked along the footpath that cuts alongside the old walls said that she came so close to him that he heard her silk dress rustle. Fortunately for him, she passed him by without a second look. For it is her glance that brings bad luck.

For centuries the enigmatic lady in black has been visiting the castle site. Then, in 1947, came a startling discovery. As the old ruins were being passed from private hands to those of the Ministry of Works, now English Heritage, some archaeological digs were undertaken. Most of what was found proved to be mundane domestic pottery and rubbish, but one excavation revealed a long forgotten cellar. And in the small, shallow, brick-lined cavity lay a badly decomposed skeleton.

Is this the last remains of some poor soul done to death long ago in the dank dungeons of the castle? If so it may explain the unquiet wanderings of the lady in black and why she exhibits such animosity to the present-day inhabitants of Hartshill.

ASTLEY

Ambition, greed and treachery feature in the story of the first of the hauntings to be encountered at Astley. The tale involves two ghosts that flit about the castle ruins. In reality the building was always more of a fortified manor house than a true castle, its comfortable rooms providing luxurious living to generations of the Grey family.

It was in 1553 that fate caught up with the Greys. They had been living prosperous, but relatively quiet, lives for generations. Then Henry Grey married Frances, daughter of the Duke of Suffolk and granddaughter of Mary, sister of King Henry VIII. The marriage brought some wealth, though not much, and family links to court and crown. It seemed a good idea at the time. Then came a succession of early deaths, executions and banishments among the royal family and higher nobility. By the fateful year, Henry's daughter Jane Grey was fourth in line to the throne.

It was becoming quickly clear that the teenage King Edward VI was dying of consumption. Officially his heir was his sister, the Catholic Mary, but the Protestants believed she was illegitimate. After Mary came another sister, the Protestant Elizabeth, but the Catholics declared that she was illegitimate. The only heir both Catholics and Protestants could accept as legitimate was young Jane Grey, then just fifteen years old.

John Dudley, Duke of Northumberland, was by this time the head of government. He was ambitious for his family and arranged a marriage between his son, Guildford Dudley, and Jane Grey. He thus brought his family directly into royal circles, and promised Henry Grey a great deal of patronage as a reward for bullying his daughter into the marriage. But he had higher ambitions. He wanted to keep the crown in Protestant hands, preferably his own. He planned to get rid of both Mary and Elizabeth and instead put Jane on the throne. He hoped to rule through his daughter-in-law.

Then King Edward died. Northumberland moved fast. He announced that the dying king had left the crown to Jane Grey, as the only undisputedly legitimate heir, and produced a piece of paper signed to that effect. The law officers of the court declared it was illegal as it had not been witnessed by the correct persons, but Northumberland's sword persuaded them to endorse it. Northumberland then sent for Mary, Elizabeth and Jane. Mary refused, Elizabeth sent a note saying she was ill and only Jane turned up. When told that she was now queen, Jane fainted. When she came to, she said that Mary was the true queen, but later she was forced to agree.

Princess Mary, meanwhile, had been gathering supporters and an army. When she set out for London the citizens turned against the corrupt Northumberland and poor Jane Grey, whom they saw as his stooge. Just nine days after being declared queen, Jane Grey surrendered to Mary and begged for mercy. Poor Lady Jane was promptly tried for treason, found guilty and sentenced to death. But Mary gave her the promised mercy and sent her to prison instead of the scaffold.

And then Jane's father, Henry Grey, came back into the story. Among Mary's first acts as queen were bringing in Catholic priests, celebrating Catholic mass and arranging to marry the King of Spain. Protestant opinion was outraged and a rebellion gathered in the midlands. Henry Grey joined the rebels and marched towards London. Mary's professional soldiers put the uprising down amid much bloodshed.

Henry Grey fled, but his actions had been enough to convince Mary that Jane had to die. On 12 February 1554 the young girl was taken from her rooms at the Tower and beheaded. Her father, meanwhile, had fled to Astley where he hid in a tree. Food and drink were carried to the fugitive by a servant named Underwood. One day, however, Underwood brought the queen's soldiers rather than food. Grey was arrested, taken to London and executed. The oak in which he had hidden stood just outside the churchyard until 1891, when it came down in a storm.

The phantoms of a father and daughter haunt the ruins of Astley Castle.

It is the ghosts of this unhappy father and daughter who are spotted at the castle. As befits her studious, religious character, Jane sits reading quietly. Before the castle was gutted by fire, visitors used to mistake the ghost for some local girl in odd costume. These days she seems quite out of place among the gaunt stones and, when she appears, is seen for what she is.

There is no mistaking her father's phantom for anything other than a ghost. In time honoured fashion he is said to appear headless as he walks around the castle ruins. Unlike the ghost of Jane Grey, however, there are no recent sightings of the ghostly Henry. Perhaps he has ceased his spectral wanderings.

St Mary the Virgin in Astley is haunted by an enigmatic ghost.

Very much still around, however, is the enigmatic phantom seen in and around the churchyard of St Mary the Virgin, Astley. This figure appears briefly among the gravestones, walking with head bowed beneath a hood or cowl. He is not viewed for long, and very often vanishes almost as soon as he is noticed. Although known locally as the ghost monk, there is little evidence that he really is, or rather was, a monk. He is as likely to be a vicar – or even some entirely secular local who wears a hooded cloak.

The truth may never be known.

WOLVEY

The month of July is the time to come to Wolvey in search of the supernatural, for this is the anniversary of a tragic event that was to claim three lives.

Back in the 18th century a local man fell in love with a girl from a passing group of gypsies. The villagers warned him that no good would come of the romance, for the travellers would soon move on. The man was, however, truly smitten as was the girl. To the surprise of almost everyone, the girl gave up her travelling life to marry the man and settle down in Wolvey, but the following July tragedy struck. The beautiful girl died in childbirth, the baby dying also.

The pair were buried together in the same grave in Wolvey churchyard. Every day the distraught young man would come to the grave on his way to and from work, weeping for the loved ones he had lost. A year to the day since the burial, he was found dead, slumped over the grave. His family buried him in the same grave as his wife and baby.

The churchyard at Wolvey, where a tragedy of long ago has led to a persistent haunting.

Each July the young couple, carrying their baby in their arms, return to the churchyard. They are seen sitting or walking quietly and appear to be quite at peace with themselves and with the world that treated them all so badly.

COVENTRY

The historic heart of Coventry was torn out on the night of 14 November 1940. The city had seen wars come and go, plagues ravage its population and economic declines but nothing was as devastating to its fabric as that single terrible night.

The raid had been ordered by German dictator Adolf Hitler after the dogged defiance of the pilots of the RAF had forced him to call off his planned invasion of Britain. Instead, Hitler decided to pound Britain to surrender, or at least to impotence, by heavy and sustained bombing of key areas. Several cities had been struck when Luftwaffe Chief Hermann Goering drew up a new plan codenamed 'Moonlight Sonata'. This called for almost 500 bombers to drop 500 tons of high explosive and 900 canisters of incendiaries on a city centre. The raid was to be given added potency by the use of a revolutionary navigation system that would ensure few aircraft lost their way.

Coventry was chosen as the target for Moonlight Sonata, largely because it had not been much bombed and so the city centre was packed with undamaged factories, housing and other areas. Given the scale of the raid it is surprising that there were not more casualties than the 550 people killed and 1,200 wounded. Over 60,000 buildings were destroyed, including the medieval cathedral.

After the war the city centre was rebuilt. It was decided to keep the gaunt cathedral ruins standing, exactly as they had been left by the German bombers. A new cathedral was built nearby. For some years after the war, shift workers and others passing the cathedral around 2 am, the time the bombers struck, reported odd happenings. Some heard the sound of droning aircraft engines overhead, others saw searchlights probing the black sky, and a few were aware of the sounds of explosions and pounding guns as if from a great distance. It was widely believed that these were the ghosts of that terrible night. As traffic levels

The shattered ruins of Coventry Cathedral have been preserved as they were on the morning after the devastating Luftwaffe raid of 14 November 1940, which has led to the haunting of the site.

increased and night-long traffic noise filled the city centre the ghostly sightings became fewer. That is not to say that the ghosts of Coventry's destruction no longer return, only that they can no longer be heard.

The German bombing destroyed most of the ancient centre of Coventry, and took the city's ghosts with it. If any survived the reduction to rubble of the pubs, houses and streets that they haunted, they did not endure past the rebuilding of the 1950s. Beyond the bombed area, however, there are ghosts to be found.

Spon Street lies just off the Ringway, west of the city centre. Several of the shops in this street have been frequented by a phantom lady wearing a long black dress with a whitish bodice. One witness said she had dark hair pulled up and tied into a bun, though others have reported that she has short hair. This particular ghost is associated with a heavy perfume that will fill the air for no apparent reason, then dissipate just as quickly. Sometimes the ghost will be seen and the scent smelled together, but more often the two will occur separately. Perhaps this means that the ghost is present, but goes unseen, when the scent pervades the air.

The cellar beneath the city's Tourist Information Bureau has long had a reputation for being haunted, though actual sightings are rarely reported. More

The very modern Aston Court Hotel is reported to be haunted by several ghosts, at least one of which dates back to the older buildings that stood on this site.

commonly said to be experienced are feelings of unease and a sense of being watched by unseen eyes. Several people have felt distinctly uncomfortable in the place and more than one has refused to return.

In the year 2000 the site was investigated by researchers from Coventry University using a wide variety of equipment. The most interesting finding was that the cellar experienced several short bursts of low-level infrasound of about 19Hz and 38 decibels. This was far below the range audible to humans, but at a level that is know to affect some people quite seriously. Workers exposed to machinery emitting infrasound around 19Hz can become nauseous and generally unwell. Is this a haunting that is caused by some distant machinery emitting sub-audible sound? It is at least a possibility.

The Aston Court Hotel in Holyhead Road lays claim to no fewer than five phantoms, and has been the site of an investigation by the Ghost Society of

England. Four of the ghosts are fairly inoffensive and inactive spectres who are rarely seen and cause no real disturbance. Rather different is the ghostly maid who appears upstairs. She was, apparently, badly treated by the manager of the hotel many years ago and has taken a dislike to men. She is known to hide tools or other small objects that belong to men, but not to women, and has been blamed when a man trips up or has a small accident in the haunted part of the hotel. Generally, however, she is little trouble. Certainly she does nothing to detract from the welcoming atmosphere and fine hospitality of the hotel.

In passing it is worth noting that the open land and woods of the Chapelfields suburb have recently been the scene for sightings of a gigantic black cat-like creature. Whether this creature is a real life big cat or a supernatural apparition is unclear. Certainly no zoo or private collection has reported a leopard or panther to be missing, but the sightings seem more likely to refer to a living creature than a ghost. Two teenage boys saw the creature at a range of just six feet. The description they gave resembles that of a leopard, but the cat is elusive and gives the impression of being able to vanish almost at will.

Coventry is surely a city of mysteries.

CANLEY

There are many haunted pubs in England, but few are named after their ghost. The Phantom Coach at Canley is one of the exceptions.

The ghost is much older than the pub, dating back at least two centuries. In those days the wide dual carriageway that is now the A45 trunk route between Birmingham and Northampton was merely a local track, as was the road that crossed it heading south from Coventry. The land around the crossroads was boggy, marshy and devoid of human habitation.

Exactly what happened here late one foggy night is not known for certain as there were no survivors. A stagecoach failed to arrive at its destination, and search parties were sent out next morning. They found the tracks left by horses' hooves and coach wheels leaving the road near this spot and disappearing into the treacherous bogs. There was no sign of the coach, horses or passengers, though bits and pieces of broken coachwork turned up over the following years.

Soon after the accident, travellers making their way along these lonely roads at night reported seeing a coach driving past at high speed. The horses were being whipped to a gallop by a frenzied man standing in the driving seat and wielding a whip over his head. The coach dashed by with lamps gleaming and passengers screaming in fear and alarm. Had the coach driver gone mad and driven his vehicle to destruction? We will never know, but if the ghostly coach is anything to go by some such gruesome and terrifying event must have taken place.

Since the A45 became a dual carriageway, the ghost has not been seen much. Perhaps the bright electric streetlights and continually passing motor traffic have finally put it off. After all, this is no longer a remote and bleak landscape, but a part of the ever growing suburbs of Coventry.

BAGINTON

The charming village of Baginton is a strangely isolated place, though it lies barely three miles from the centre of Coventry. The thundering main roads of the A45, A46, A423 and A445 surround the settlement and almost cut it off. The three ghostly ladies may prefer it that way.

It was not always like this. Baginton stands astride one of the most ancient roads in Britain. Running north-west to south-east, the road crossed the River Sowe by way of a ford just upstream of the modern bridge at Baginton. It was certainly in use 12,000 years ago, for Neolithic stone tools have been found here. Later, the Romans built a small fortress, now partially reconstructed as a tourist attraction, to guard the river crossing.

The crossing likewise attracted the medieval Bagget, or Bagot, family who built a castle south-east of the ford in 1232. The castle saw action in 1395 when the family joined the nobles who were trying to rein in the profligate, corrupt and increasingly cruel Richard II, but Coventry sided with the king. After seeing more action in the Wars of the Roses, the castle was abandoned when

The young lady who has been seen at the ruined castle of Baginton has a sad history.

cannon made stout stone walls useless in war. The Bagget family moved to a comfortable manor elsewhere and Baginton Castle fell into utter ruin. In 1934 a group of amateur archaeologists from Coventry came to excavate the site. They got rather more than they expected.

Soon after they began digging, the excavators realised that they were being cold-shouldered by some of the older residents of the village. The trouble, it soon emerged, was the fear that the digging would anger the 'poor lady of the castle'. It was said that this ghost was that of a beautiful young heiress who had been kidnapped at some unknown date in the past by a rapacious young Bagget knight. He had held her prisoner in Baginton Castle until she agreed to marry him and so bring her vast acres and wealth to the Bagget family. The girl refused and died sad and alone.

Apparently she took a grudge against the villagers of Baginton who had done nothing to help her. After her death she returned to stalk the castle and the surrounding lands, although she had not been seen for some years before the excavation. There were stories that the ghost walked again while the digging was in progress, but now she seems to have vanished once more. It is to be hoped the unfortunate girl has found peace.

Rather more active is the phantom lady in the cloak who haunts the church and rectory. In some ways this spectre is what people expect a ghost to be. She appears with some frequency, follows the same route every time she walks and moves with an eerie glide over paths, grass and road, and through a gate. To add to the classic nature of the phantom, she is said to be semi-transparent.

The Old Mill Hotel at Baginton has a ghost that must be among
the most active in Warwickshire.

She proceeds out of the church, down the path and out of the churchyard to cross the road. Some say that she then enters the garden of the Old Rectory opposite, though she sometimes fades from view before getting this far. Enigmatically, nobody knows anything about the story behind this ghost.

Rather more is known about the third ghostly lady of Baginton, who haunts the Old Mill Hotel down by the river. A mill has stood on this spot since at least the 11th century, for it is recorded in the Domesday Book. The present structure is, of course, much younger but is nonetheless several centuries old. The hotel consists of the old mill and a 17th century house, to which it is linked by modern infill, and a very modern bedroom wing that has been carefully designed to blend in.

The modern building has clearly been done with some skill for it has not disturbed the most ancient inhabitant of the hotel. This sad phantom was murdered here many generations ago – quite how many is not clear – and her shade has clung to the place ever since. She is seen at her best on the spiral staircase in the old house. This flight of stairs is one of only two in England that make two complete revolutions from top to bottom. The lady, dressed in a long dress of pale colour, walks demurely down the staircase towards what is now the main dining area of the hotel, but was formerly the entrance hall of the house.

When seen here, the ghost remains in view for some time and can be clearly distinguished. Her dress would seem to date her to about the early 18th century. Despite the firm local belief that the ghost is the spectre of a murder victim, there were no murders recorded here during these years. Perhaps the lady suffered a death in circumstances that caused local gossip to talk of murder when official documents recorded disease or accident.

But the ghost does not only appear on the spiral staircase. Staff at the hotel report that she is seen more often on the ground floor and through into what was formerly the mill. She is not visible so clearly here, nor for as long. She is usually glimpsed as a moving figure out of the corner of the eye, but has vanished if the person turns to see who is there. This can be particularly unnerving late at night when all is quiet and still, when nobody should be about and only the ghost walks to disturb the peace of the night.

A short distance from the Old Mill Hotel stands the bridge, which has replaced the age-old ford across the River Sowe. Something unpleasant is said to lurk here, though quite what is uncertain. 'I wouldn't walk by there after dark' is a typical comment. There may have been a road accident some years back that has left a nasty memory.

COOMBE ABBEY

The imposing mansion and park of Coombe Abbey are looked after by Coventry City Council and can be visited free of charge, though much of the house is now occupied by a hotel.

The property was founded as a Cistercian abbey in 1150 by Richard de Camville – he married the widow of Sir Robert Marmion, who famously tried to close down Polesworth Abbey but failed. At one time it was the richest

The main gates to Coombe Abbey, the scene of more than one haunting.

establishment in Warwickshire, but later fell into debt and put up little resistance when it was closed down by Henry VIII in 1539.

Turned into a private house, the building has been remodelled and restored so often that little of its Tudor fabric remains. Probably the most famous resident was Princess Elizabeth, daughter of King James I. In 1605 the 9-year-old girl was suddenly plunged into great danger. The conspirators in what became known as the Gunpowder Plot planned to exterminate the entire royal family in London. Little Princess Elizabeth in Warwickshire was to be seized and forced at swordpoint to accept both the crown and the Catholic government demanded by the plotters.

On 5 November 1605 armed men rode to Coombe Abbey to seize the little girl, but the Earl of Harrington was the girl's guardian and a man of action. He roused his servants to hold off the plotters while someone rode to Coventry. There the alarm was given and a force of loyal citizens galloped out to attack the conspirators. The running fight covered miles of countryside until the rebels were caught or killed. All were later executed.

The stretch of road outside Coombe Abbey where a sedate phantom cycles by.

Little Princess Elizabeth later grew into a noted beauty. She married well, becoming Queen of Bohemia and mother of Prince Rupert. This dashing Cavalier would later feature in the haunting of Edgehill battlefield, but it is unclear whether his mother is the phantom who lurks at Coombe Abbey.

This particular phantom is glimpsed very rarely, so a positive identification is not possible. She is certainly a teenage girl, or at least a slight young lady, and her long dress with wide skirts may date her to the time when young Princess Elizabeth lived here. She is heard, and sometimes seen, running across the courtyard of the house.

Another phantom at Coombe Abbey is very definitely better avoided. In the days when Lord Leofric held sway over the lands around Coventry, and his lovely wife Lady Godiva prepared for her famous naked ride through the city, the lake at Coombe was famous for its large, tasty fish. One particular day a young farmhand was fishing there when he hooked what seemed to be a truly enormous fish. After an exhausting struggle, the lad was amazed to find that he had landed a breathtakingly beautiful woman. As the two youngsters surveyed each other, and the startled young man began to realise he had landed a water nymph, there was a blinding flash of light.

Leaping into view came the Devil himself. The details of what followed are understandably hazy. The upshot, however, was clear. The farmboy married the nymph while the waters of the pond remained the abode of the Devil. To this day the evil one may decide to appear here if anyone takes more than their due from his domain.

The ghost that has been seen on the main road outside the abbey is altogether more gentle. She is an elderly lady, dressed in a warm tweed skirt of very sensible cut. She rides an old-fashioned lady's bicycle with high handlebars and wide mudguards. This particular spectre cycles along as if she is without a care in the world, ignoring any motorists or mortal cyclists who try to use the road. Who she is and why she rides so serenely past the abbey remain total mysteries.

BRANDON

t is not the village of Brandon itself that is haunted, but the main road running east towards Rugby. And a most unnerving phantom this is. Just outside the village the main road makes a sudden and extremely sharp turn to the right. This is not the only tight corner on this road – which may explain why this is no longer the main Coventry to Rugby through route – but it is the one that has caused the haunting.

The sharp corner on the main road just outside Brandon
that has become the site of a dramatic haunting.

In the 1950s a lorry was heading out of Brandon on a foggy night at what was to prove to be a dangerously high speed. Nobody knows quite what happened as the driver was killed in the accident that followed. For whatever reason, the lorry careered off the road at the corner and overturned. No other vehicle seems to have been involved in the accident. But it is other vehicles that are being involved in the phantom recreation of that original crash.

Drivers heading west along this stretch of road after dark are sometimes confronted by an old-fashioned lorry hurtling towards them at high speed. With headlights blazing, the vehicle seems to be dangerously out of control. It goes from side to side, skids, turns violently and threatens instant collision. Some drivers have swerved to avoid a crash; others have slammed on their brakes. But the alarming apparition suddenly vanishes as if the vehicle has plunged off the road. Most drivers then halt and get out of their vehicles to locate the tangled wreckage they expect to result from the high speed crash they think they have witnessed. But there is never anything there. The crash happened over 50 years ago and it is the ghost, not the twisted metal, that remains.

•West Warwickshire•

KENILWORTH

The towering ruins of Kenilworth Castle demonstrate the power
and wealth that once resided here.

Time was when Kenilworth was the most prosperous, fashionable and important town in Warwickshire. But those days are now long gone, for the prestige of the town was built not on any inherent economic foundations, but on the wealth and power of the family that owned Kenilworth Castle.

This castle was one of the largest and most sturdily built in the kingdom. The fortress was begun in 1112 by Geoffrey de Clinton, Chamberlain to King Henry I. Clinton's son erected the massive stone keep that still dominates the place and fifty years later King John lavished £2,000 on making this a state of the art fortification surrounded by double walls and a vast artificial lake. By the time the work was finished in 1210, Kenilworth was effectively impregnable. Its greatest siege came in 1266 when the supporters of Simon de Montfort, Earl of Leicester, held out against King Henry III for nine months and surrendered only when on the point of starvation.

After the invention of gunpowder made mighty stone walls ineffective in war, Kenilworth was transformed into a sumptuous palace where royalty stayed on their visits to the area. In 1558 it came into the hands of Robert Dudley, Earl of Leicester, who at once lavished vast sums on the place to make it the most magnificent private house in England.

Although his father had been executed by Queen Mary for treason, young Robert was excused and later became a favourite of Queen Elizabeth I. His good looks, witty conversation and undoubted gallantry made Leicester popular in the country as well as with Elizabeth. His prospects of marrying the queen were rather spoilt by the fact that he was already married, to Amy Robsart. When his wife died suddenly after a mysterious fall downstairs, Leicester was widely suspected of murder. Although Elizabeth was forced to drop him as a possible husband, he remained a favourite, and she came to Kenilworth to enjoy his lavish hospitality.

Kenilworth's glory days were, by now, numbered. In the Civil War the castle declared for the King, and was pounded to ruin by Cromwell's artillery. Fragments of the fortress remained habitable, however, and continued to be lived in over the years. One of these parts was the gatehouse, now used for recitals, exhibitions and the like. It is here that the ghost of Kenilworth Castle is to be encountered.

She is a gentle soul, a lady in her twenties who sits quietly beside one of the windows on the first floor of the building. She ignores all those about her as she gazes out across the town of Kenilworth, so greatly changed since her day, and from time to time bends to attend to some task in her lap. One witness thought that the phantom was sewing, but another said she was reading a book. Whatever her occupation, it is clearly quite absorbing.

The clothes of the ghost seem to date her to the later medieval period, perhaps around 1380 or so. There is no hint as to the identity of this serene young lady, but this was a date when Kenilworth Castle was enjoying some decades of peace and security. Quite clearly she is happy here.

A second apparition to haunt the castle is a coach and four that gallops out of the old southern gateway, thundering over the embankment that was once a causeway over the lake and disappearing towards Warwick at high speed. Again, the identity of the phantom coach and its inhabitants are utterly obscure. Since the vision is seen only very rarely it seems unlikely the mystery will be solved.

Just as Kenilworth Castle was once one of the finest in England, so too was Kenilworth Priory one of the largest in the kingdom. This was founded in 1122 by the same Geoffrey de Clinton who first built the castle. Presumably he wanted to ensure both his worldly safety and spiritual sanctity by these twin foundations so close to each other. By 1450 the Priory had become so large and wealthy that the Pope raised it to the status of an abbey and gave its prior the status of abbot – then a privilege well worth having within the Catholic Church.

In 1538 the abbey was closed down, along with all the others in England, by King Henry VIII as part of his establishment of the Protestant Church in his kingdom. The vast complex of buildings was mostly demolished and the materials sold off for profit within a year or two; a 10 hundredweight ingot made of lead melted from the roof was found buried in the field and is now in the church. The foundations, however, were left behind as they were too difficult to dig out. The great open space of Abbey Fields now covers these foundations, providing a welcome open park to the people of Kenilworth.

In the 1880s the site was fully excavated and the diggers were surprised by how much of the old abbey church still remained. The ruins of this building have been left exposed and now form part of the churchyard to the town's parish church of St Nicholas. The location of the buried ruins can have come as no surprise to the townsfolk, however. For centuries a procession of phantom monks has left the west door of the parish church and marched slowly along the

The avenue of trees along which process the phantom monks of Kenilworth.

avenue of trees that leads down to Abbey Fields. At the end of the avenue, the procession turns left and continues for a few yards before vanishing. The spot where it disappears was revealed during the excavations to be the main entrance to the abbey church. Clearly the ghostly monks knew where they were going.

Some people have claimed to hear the faint sounds of chanting and choral singing while resting in the old ruined church. These phantom echoes of long ago seem to come and go. They were especially active in the late 1970s then faded for a while before returning in the 1990s. No visible ghosts accompany the eerie monkish chanting from so long ago, and the sounds do not last for very long. By the time a person has taken in what they are hearing, looked around for somebody with a radio and realised there is no such easy explanation, the singing has gone.

Unlike the ghosts, which remain.

GUY'S CLIFFE

There is not much to show that Blacklow Hill, above Guy's Cliffe, was the scene for one of the key acts of brutal violence in the history of medieval England. It was an event that sent ripples of disorder across England, which lasted for years.

The countdown to tragedy began on 20 July 1307 when King Edward II sent a message to France asking the young nobleman Piers Gaveston to return to England. At the time Edward was 23 years old and had just inherited the kingdom from his father, Edward I. He was tall, handsome and witty, but disastrously indecisive and weak-willed. He had for some years relied upon the slightly older and more forceful Gaveston to run his household and offer him advice. But when Edward I realised the two young men were gay lovers, he had sent Gaveston to exile in France. Now Gaveston was back.

Edward made his lover, Earl of Cornwall, and lavished lands and wealth upon him. This was not enough for Gaveston, who persuaded Edward to give him authority over tax collection. Soon tax moneys were being siphoned off into the pockets of Gaveston, while Edward demanded that more taxes be levied to restore the royal finances. Edward would, of course, have nothing bad said about Gaveston and refused even to look at evidence of his financial misdoings.

Other favourites had been given wealth by their royal lovers, but Gaveston inspired a hatred and loathing that was unique. He was undoubtedly clever and witty, but used his wit in cruel jests and barbed comments at every opportunity. He mocked the most powerful men and women quite openly in public. He even threw casual insults at quite blameless citizens if he thought it would raise a laugh – and nobody laughed more at Gaveston's jokes than did Gaveston himself.

On one occasion he tousled the long, black hair of the Earl of Warwick and called him 'My black dog of Arden'. Warwick was furious. 'I'll show him how a dog bites,' he shouted and drew his sword. Only the rapid intervention of nearby knights held him back. The Earl of Warwick was a proud man with great wealth and enormous power. He never forgave this very public insult.

In 1308 Warwick persuaded his fellow noblemen to put an ultimatum to the king. Gaveston had to be exiled or no taxes would be paid. Faced by a united front, Edward gave in and sent his lover back to France. But in July 1309 Gaveston returned. Edward had won Parliament, representing the merchants and gentry, to his cause by reforming tax collection and other abuses. He had also persuaded several magnates that Warwick was getting too powerful.

Gaveston was kept away from the royal finances this time, but he found it impossible to keep silent. He dubbed the Duke of Lancaster 'The Fiddler' as if he were a common minstrel and insulted an entire noble dynasty by referring to a rumour by repeatedly calling the Duke of Gloucester 'whore's son' as if he were illegitimate and his wealthy mother were a prostitute. Gradually Edward's supporters fell away in their hatred of bold, witty, handsome Gaveston. In July 1312 they struck.

The Earl of Pembroke grabbed Gaveston at Scarborough when Edward was, for once, not present. Pembroke told Gaveston he would be sent into exile, but would be executed if he ever returned. Having got Gaveston under lock and key, Pembroke set off for London to join a council of nobles that was preparing to formalise Gaveston's trial and sentence. But while Pembroke rode south, Warwick and Lancaster rode north. They dragged Gaveston from his prison and took him to Warwick Castle.

When he heard the news, Pembroke turned around and led his men towards Warwick. He arrived too late. At dawn, Warwick and Lancaster had tied Gaveston to a horse. To mock him the mount was gaily dressed with ribbons and bells. Followed by a mob of citizens, the noblemen led Gaveston to Blacklow Hill, which lay just outside Warwick's lands. There a soldier hacked off Gaveston's head. There had not even been the pretence of a trial.

Edward never forgot nor forgave the murder. From then on his rule was dedicated to the secret, careful trapping of his enemies. The war with Scotland was lost as the king was too busy to pay proper attention. The rule of law crumbled while Edward ignored the problems. Warwick died a natural death, but others in the conspiracy were gradually isolated then arrested on trumped up charges to be imprisoned, fined or executed. Finally, in 1322, Edward got Lancaster. The Earl had been foolish enough to correspond with King Robert of Scotland. When Edward was passed the letters bearing Lancaster's own signature and seal he at once hauled the Earl up for trial on charges of treason. The verdict was 'guilty' and Lancaster was beheaded just minutes later.

Edward himself did not survive long. He was murdered by his own wife and her lover, supported by all those suffering because the king had abandoned the business of ruling his kingdom to pursue his personal vendetta of violence.

Through all this time the bare hillside above Guy's Cliffe had been left bleak and lonely. King and nobles ignored the site of Gaveston's murder, but the local peasants could not. For time and again a tall, handsome man with his hands tied behind him was seen to ride up from Warwick along the track that leads to the top of the hill. Beside him marched armed men. The only sound to be heard was the mournful jingling of the bells with which the horse was bedecked.

The sad ghost of Piers Gaveston being led to his murder has continued to be seen over the years. Recently the main road from Coventry to the south, the A46, has been diverted around northern Warwick, cutting deep into Blacklow Hill and blocking the track up to the high ground from Warwick. These days the ghostly procession seems to have abandoned the southern part of its sad journey. It is now seen only on the hillside itself, and on the spot where murder was committed so many years ago.

WARWICK

The ancient county town of Warwick was already old when Queen Ethelflaeda of Mercia, daughter of King Alfred the Great, erected a fortress on the hill to defend the bridge over the Avon against the Vikings. Since then the castle has dominated the town, as it still does.

Although the site dates back to the 9th century, none of the castle buildings are older than the 13th century. Each generation updated the castle to take account of the latest in military engineering, and it also became a splendid stately home. The ghost that lurks here belongs to the period when harsh military necessity was giving way to luxurious living.

Sir Fulke Greville was the very image of a successful Elizabethan Englishman. He was born into the gentry, to a family wealthy enough to send him to Cambridge to be educated. His skill as a poet gained him the attention of the courtier Sir Philip Sidney. Once mixing at court, Greville impressed all who met him with his skills at accountancy and handling money. In 1583 Queen Elizabeth made him Secretary of Wales, and he never looked back. Greville managed to win favour with the new king, James I, after Elizabeth's death and

Warwick Castle is the scene of a haunting caused by a murder over 400 years ago.

in 1614 he rose to become the Chancellor of England. He had come a long way, showing that ability and talent could bring rich rewards even to those of relatively humble birth. In 1621, at the age of 68, Greville retired from public life and the grateful monarch created him Baron Brooke.

Throughout his time working for the government, Greville had kept up his writings. He produced over a hundred sonnets and several longer poems. His authorship of two plays did not become public until after his death, though both had been successful when produced anonymously around 1608.

In 1612 Greville bought Warwick Castle, then in a fairly rundown condition. He lavished his wealth upon the pile, converting it into a beautiful mansion with all the latest conveniences. Most luxurious of all were the private apartments he made for himself and his wife in the Watergate Tower.

It was there, on a fateful night in 1628, that the aging Greville wrote out his will. The lawyer who set down Sir Fulke's wishes in the technical legal talk of the period insisted that the document had to be witnessed in his presence. Sir Fulke sent for two of his servants who he knew could read and write.

One of these servants was Thomas Haywood, who had served Greville faithfully from his earliest days as a struggling poet hoping to be noticed. As was soon to become clear, Haywood was under the impression that he was to be left a tidy sum by Sir Fulke in his will. Now called upon to witness the document he took the opportunity to scan it to see what he would receive. Unfortunately, Sir Fulke was not planning to leave him anything, believing his wages had been thanks enough for the work done.

Haywood flew into a rage, shouting at his master in most un-servantlike language. Before anyone could restrain him, the man had snatched up the lawyer's penknife and plunged it deep into Sir Fulke's chest. The man then fled. Sir Fulke died quickly. A search for the murderer found him, also dead, from a self-inflicted cut throat.

Sir Fulke's body was taken to his hometown of Alcester where it was interred in a beautiful and impressive tomb. His ghost, however, remains at Warwick Castle; the suite of rooms in the Watergate Tower is the scene of the haunting. Sir Fulke is seen dressed in his comfortable, but still elegant retirement clothes. He potters about quietly and bothers nobody, though he does give a start to people who come across him unexpectedly.

Warwick Castle is now operated as a tourist attraction, rather than a fortress or courtier's home. The grisly death of Sir Fulke is recreated in the form of waxworks, while the ghostly manifestations are conjured up with some spine-tingling visual trickery – this is one of the few ghosts in England to feature in reality almost as often as in special effects.

Altogether more alarming is the phantom that prowls the narrow lanes around the castle. These twisting thoroughfares follow the layout of the old medieval town that sprang up in the shelter of the hilltop fortress, though few of the buildings are even half as old as the roads they line. In 1694 a fire broke out here that spread rapidly. The flames engulfed street after street and lapped up against the stone walls of the castle itself. By the time the desperate townsfolk had managed to quench the fires, over 250 houses had been reduced to ashes along with much of St Mary's church. Most of the town centre dates from the rebuilding that followed.

But if the good citizens of Warwick hoped that the fire had rid them of their most troublesome supernatural resident, they were sadly mistaken.

In the 13th century the then Earl of Warwick rewarded an elderly servant by the name of Moll Bloxham by giving her a monopoly on selling milk within the town walls of Warwick. To doubly ensure she had a comfortable retirement, the Earl instructed his cook to give Moll any milk left over in the castle kitchens at the end of each day. This she could churn into butter for sale.

Old Moll did very well out of the deal, but not well enough. The housewives of Warwick began to notice that milk ladled out by Moll Bloxham did not fill their jugs quite as full as it should. They complained to the Earl, who came to Moll's cottage in these lanes in person, accompanied by his cook. Together they seized Moll's pint ladle and compared it to the cook's measure. It was, indeed, short of a pint by some considerable amount. The Earl, angered by the abuse of his gift, threw Moll out of her house and ordered her to be forever banished from Warwick.

One of the ancient, narrow lanes in Warwick haunted by the troublesome phantom of Moll Bloxham.

The old woman spat at him, then cursed the Earl and the town in general. She shouted hideous abuse, then promised to be back and vowed that the town would never be rid of her. The rather alarmed soldiers hurried her out of the town gates at swordpoint and watched as she tottered off down the high road.

That very night Moll Bloxham came home, but not as a doddery old woman. She returned in the form of a hideous hell hound. Standing four feet tall, the great black dog came trotting up the road along which the wicked old woman had left a few hours earlier. Reaching the town gate, it leapt bodily over the towering wooden doors, terrifying the watchman on duty, then ran into the maze of narrow lanes.

Night after night the immense black dog was seen prowling the dark alleys of medieval Warwick. And one by one the people who had complained about Moll's milk measure were found dead. Believing that it would not be long before he too was sent to his death by the vengeful hound, the Earl ordered the three vicars of Warwick to perform an exorcism. As dusk fell, the clergymen met to summon up the evil spirit and send it back to Hell. They brought the dog to them without any trouble, and managed to hold it at bay with bell, book and candle. But no matter what incantation the holy men tried they could not send the dog away. Then one remembered that Moll had promised she would never leave Warwick. Instead of sending the dog to Hell, the clergymen sent it to the deep dungeons beneath the Caesar Tower of the castle, binding it with sacred vows to remain in its prison.

The great black dog of Warwick does, as a rule, stay in its sealed up subterranean prison. But there is the odd night when it breaks its bonds and once again prowls the narrow, twisting streets of central Warwick. Those who turned Moll out of her home are long dead, and the black dog no longer inflicts sudden death on those it encounters. Instead, it contents itself with doling out a remarkably unhealthy dose of bad luck. For a year and a day after seeing the gigantic dog, a person will have no good fortune at love or at work.

So, should anyone hear the soft padding of paws on cobblestones or become aware of the approaching pant of some large beast, it is probably wise to walk briskly in the opposite direction. These may not be streets to hang around in late at night.

BADDESLEY CLINTON

The little village of Baddesley Clinton has more than its fair share of ghosts, most of them linked to the Brome-Ferrers family who were lords of the manor from 1438 to 1940.

The oldest ghost here is that of Nicholas Brome, who inherited the house in 1483. This was just as the Wars of the Roses were coming to an end. The Bromes had taken the side of the claimants to the throne from the House of York while their neighbour, the Squire of Longbridge, had taken the side of Lancaster. With the final Lancastrian victory of 1483, Longbridge had taken the opportunity to settle, as he thought, a long running land dispute by ambushing and killing Nicholas's father. Longbridge relied upon the fact that the new Lancastrian king, Henry Tudor, would overlook the killing of a Yorkist supporter in the days of turmoil surrounding the seizure of the throne.

The church tower at Baddesley Clinton. Nicholas Brome is buried beneath the door.

King Henry did overlook the matter, but young Nicholas Brome did not. On hearing that royal justice would not avenge his father's death, Nicholas mounted his horse and galloped off to Longbridge. There he boldly rode into the courtyard, cut down all who opposed him and killed the squire before hacking his way out again. This time the King did step in, clamping down on all violence before a dangerous feud got out of hand. Nicholas paid a heavy fine, then went home.

A few years later Nicholas was again involved in deadly violence. This time he came home late one night after dining at a friend's house, during the course of which he had indulged in some heavy drinking, to find his wife with her head on another man's shoulder. Out came the Brome sword once again and the man fell dead. Only then did Brome realise he had killed the local priest who was giving his wife some words of comfort.

This time Brome had to answer to the Church for his crimes. The result was the almost complete rebuilding of Baddesley Clinton church, which stands a short distance from Baddesley Clinton Manor. After his death, Nicholas was buried beneath the door to the church so that he would be trodden on by all worshippers as they entered and left the building.

Perhaps unsurprisingly, Nicholas Brome returns to haunt his ignominious resting place. He stalks the path up to the church through the woods and strides up to the door, beneath which he is buried, before vanishing abruptly. Traditionally he appears every ten years, his next appearance being due in 2007, but his phantom does seem to have manifested itself at other times. Certainly a tall man in medieval clothes was seen for a few seconds outside the door in 2002 by a local woman. It seems unlikely that there could be two medieval ghostly men here, so it may be that old Nicholas Brome is more active than might be thought.

The manor then passed by way of marriage to the Ferrers family. The house has been altered at various times over the years, though the original 15th century gunports commanding the front door remain. An extension was added in Georgian times, enlarging some substantial work that had been put up by Sir Henry Ferrers in the 1580s. Thereafter the Ferrers rented the property out for some decades to the Catholic Vaux family. They entertained Jesuit preachers, when such a thing was counted close to treason, and installed various hiding places about the house. Three priest holes are known, and others may exist that have not yet been discovered.

The house is believed to have two ghosts of the Ferrers family, though neither has been seen as recently as has Nicholas Brome. The older of the two is the Lady Ferrers who was seen regularly in the upper rooms between 1880 and 1920. This Lady Ferrers is believed to have resided at the house during the 1750s,

The house at Baddesley Clinton is thought to have at least two ghosts within its walls.

enjoying a long and happy life. Her ghost, complete with blue dress and long blonde hair, appeared a few times soon after her death, but then faded away. What caused the ghost to become suddenly active in the 1880s is unclear, just as is the reason for her fading again after the Great War.

Seen much less often was the ghost of Major Thomas Ferrers who died abroad. His phantom was seen a few times, but again had seemingly gone to find peace by around 1925.

Whether it is one of these ghosts, or perhaps a third, that makes the ghostly footsteps is unknown. The sounds come upstairs late at night, so it is unlikely that any modern visitors to this charming National Trust property will experience them.

Also unlikely to be seen is the ghost of a young man who appeared in the village of Baddesley Clinton on the afternoon of 16 January 1812. The young man in question, his name unfortunately was recorded merely as Mr T———, was serving with the British army under Lord Arthur Wellesley, later to become the Duke of Wellington. The army had been sent to Portugal to help fight off a French invasion. Having defeated an incursion led by the marshals of the Emperor Napoleon, Wellington prepared to march into Spain to liberate that country from the French occupation. First, however, he had to capture the fortress city of Ciudad Rodrigo, which blocked the mountain pass between the two countries.

The French garrison consisted of 2,000 men and 153 guns sheltering behind deep entrenchments and stout bastions of stone and rammed earth. Wellington's army of 35,000 men waited amid biting winds and snows while the artillery battered two breaches in the walls.

The British infantry storm the walls of Ciudad Rodrigo in 1812, a desperate battle that led to a ghost appearing in Baddesley Clinton.

Then, at 7 pm on 15 January, they attacked. About 200 men were killed and 900 wounded fighting their way into the fortress, where 300 Frenchmen died before their commander surrendered.

The following day Mrs T———, the soldier's mother, was beside the window of her cottage doing some household task or other, when she saw her son push open the front gate and walk up the path towards the cottage door. He was dressed in his uniform, though it looked worn and threadbare.

The woman was delighted. She had thought the young man was hundreds of miles away in Spain. Believing that her son must be home on unexpected leave, the mother leapt to her feet and headed for the door. When she threw it open, the path was empty. The poor woman searched the garden and surrounding streets for some time, but there was no sign of her boy.

It was some weeks before she received a letter from Spain informing her that her beloved son had been wounded in the assault on Ciudad Rodrigo and had died the next day. It would seem that he had died at more or less the moment that his mother saw his ghost walking up the garden path.

These apparitions that occur at or about the time a person dies are among the more frequent paranormal occurrences to be recorded. The most famous such event came in 1893 when Admiral Sir George Tryon – or rather his apparition – walked into his house in London at the moment his ship was sinking in the Mediterranean. The figure was seen by several servants and family members.

The mysterious appearance of young Mr T——— at Baddesley Clinton is not an isolated case.

WOOTTON WAWEN

The village of Wootton Wawen is one of the oldest in Warwickshire, and its ghosts are among the most active. There was a settlement of some sort here before the Romans came. The only trace remaining to be seen is an enigmatic turf hump in the churchyard. It may be a prehistoric burial mound, but is more likely to be a ceremonial structure of some kind. The Romans pushed their road through the place and built a staging post here, but only vague archaeological remnants tell that story.

The real glory of Wootton Wawen came during the days of the early English. This village acquired a prosperity and size that marked it out from others in this area of western Warwickshire. It also acquired a large, stone-built church that was far bigger and more impressive than the thatched wooden places of worship that served other communities in the area. Surprisingly, most of this ancient building still stands. It forms the heart of the church that continues to serve the village, though most of the fabric has been hidden behind later medieval rebuildings.

The village takes its name from Wagen, a Saxon thegn who owned the manor in the years before the Norman Conquest of 1066. What happened to Wagen is unclear, but he was certainly dead by around 1070. It is most likely that he joined the rest of the Warwickshire men who marched south in 1066 to join the English king, Harold Godwinson, as he fought against the invading Duke William of Normandy. Like Harold, Wagen must have died fighting for his nation's freedom on the bloodstained field of the Battle of Hastings. When the new Norman owners came to survey their seized lands they named the village known until then simply as Wootton, Wootton Wagen to distinguish it from all the other Woottons in England – the name later became corrupted to Wawen.

In the 12th century Wootton Wawen was given to a French Benedictine monastery by its devout owner. The French monks sent a few of their brethren to England to take possession. They were not popular. For the local English farmers it had been bad enough paying taxes to a Norman king and rents to a

The church of Wootton Wawen is the oldest in Warwickshire.

Norman landlord. But at least both of them were in England, enforcing justice and protecting the land from foreign invasion. The French monks simply took the rents and dues in kind, then sent them off to France.

Cold-shouldered by the locals, the monks built themselves a house on the field below the church and set to work gathering their rents and keeping their books. Every few months, new monks would come out from France, and the previous incumbents would go home. Inevitably the new arrivals wanted to check the books and make sure rents had been paid. The constant checking did little to endear the monks to the locals. The building was steadily enlarged until it began to be graced by the name of a priory. All things considered, it probably came as a relief to the good folk of Wootton Wawen when the priory was forcibly closed down. For once King Henry VIII was not the cause. The Bishop of Lichfield simply became exasperated with the friction between Church and laity in the village. He cut the ties to France, closed the priory and included the lands in the estates of the diocese.

The 'priory', if it ever really deserved the name, was quickly robbed of its stone by the villagers, with the once visible symbol of foreign ownership becoming built into the fabric of houses, barns and cottages throughout the village.

And yet the French monks were not gone entirely. In spectral form, they are still in Wootton Wawen. The field where they once lived is now under grass and is grazed by local farm animals. But in the cool light of dawn, mysterious shifting figures are sometimes seen flitting about the field, or processing up the hill to the parish church of St Peter. Given that the French monks cannot have been very happy here, their motive in returning so assiduously for so many centuries is unclear.

Far more obvious is the reason why the ghost of William Somerville comes this way. In fashionable, literary circles, Somerville is famous as a poet. He was born in Staffordshire in 1675, educated at Oxford, where he became a Fellow of New College, and later became the Squire of Edstone, a few miles south-east of Wootton Wawen. His poems were, and in some circles still are, highly regarded.

In Warwickshire, however, Squire Somerville was better known as a huntsman of remarkable skill and tenacity. He never missed an opportunity to

The elegant mansion at Wootton Wawen, home to more than one spectre.

mount his powerful charger and set off after the hounds, in pursuit of one of the foxes that so plagued local smallholders and their chickens. In 1735 Somerville combined his two talents by writing *The Chase*, an epic poem on the subject of hunting. For the squire it was sport, for his tenants it was pest control and for nobody – at least in those days – was it a problem.

In 1742 Somerville passed away and was buried in Wootton Wawen churchyard. But he did not rest comfortably. It took only the blast of a hunting horn to sound over his grave for the spectre of the good squire to spring from the ground, mount a spectral horse and gallop off in pursuit of the hounds. It is likely that some of the more colourful accounts of this ghost include a degree of embellishment, but there have been enough sightings of a red-faced man dressed in 18th century clothes riding the fields when the local hunt is out to make it likely that there is some truth in the story of the hunting ghost.

These days, of course, there is not so much sport for Squire Somerville to enjoy. It remains to be seen if his ghost will still ride.

Yet another resident of Wootton Wawen achieved national fame, or rather notoriety, and came back to haunt this little village. The current Wootton Hall was built in 1681 in the grand Palladian style, but it is only the latest in a succession of houses to have stood on this site since at least the time of the English thegn, Wagen. For much of that time the house has been the property of the Smythe family.

In 1643 the then Sir Charles Smythe was created Baron Carrington of Wootton by King Charles I in recognition of his loyalty during the Civil War. During the rule of Oliver Cromwell, Baron Carrington had to live abroad. As he lay dying in France he ordered that his heart be cut out and preserved until such time as his son could take it back for burial at Wootton. This was eventually made possible by the restoration to the throne of King Charles II in 1660, when he reunited the Smythe family with their estates.

The troubled spirit of Baron Carrington was for many years blamed for the tall phantom man seen in the dairy and associated outbuildings behind the Hall. But when the little complex was pulled down the bodies of a man and woman were found beneath the stone floor. Suddenly it was remembered that a son of the Catholic Smythe family had many years earlier fallen in love with one of the village girls who worked in the dairy. The girl was pretty and virtuous enough to hope that the Smythes might allow the younger son to marry beneath his station, but she was a Protestant and he a Catholic so the family frowned on the match. One day the couple vanished, and it was widely believed that they had run off to marry without family permission. The discovery made it clear that they had been murdered, perhaps by the boy's irate father though this was by no means proven. When the skeletons were given proper burial, this particular haunting ceased.

The circumstances of the mixed faith romance and its tragic aftermath makes the career of the second ghost to lurk in Wootton Hall all the more ironic. There was for many years a portrait hanging at the Hall that was thought to be that of Maria Anne Smythe, born to the Hampshire branch of the family in 1756. The young lady was said to have spent much of her childhood years here, and certainly she grew up to be intelligent, talented and remarkably attractive. At the age of 19, Maria married a Mr Edward Weld, who sadly died after falling from a horse within six months of the wedding. She married again two years later, but this husband lasted only three years until carried off by disease. Young Maria was left twice widowed at the age of only 25. She moved to Richmond in Surrey and set up house by herself, funded by the legacies of her two husbands.

It was there that Maria, now Mrs Fitzherbert, met and fell in love with Prince George, the Prince of Wales and later to be King George IV. The passion was returned and before long the two were lovers. George's passion was total, but Mrs Fitzherbert could coolly perceive the problems that lay in the path of the affair. She moved abroad, but was induced to return when the Prince fell desperately ill and summoned her to what most people thought to be his deathbed. After his recovery, the Prince insisted that he and Mrs Fitzherbert must be married.

In 1785 the marriage went ahead in secret, although under British law such a union was invalid. The relationship flourished until 1795 when the Prince was forced into a dynastic marriage to Princess Caroline of Brunswick, when Mrs Fitzherbert moved abroad. The loveless formal marriage soon foundered and the Pope was persuaded to issue a letter stating that the Protestant rites of George and Caroline were invalid, easing Mrs Fitzherbert's conscience enough to allow a rekindling of her affair. George became King in 1820 and died in 1830, Mrs Fitzherbert following him to the grave in 1837.

It is this scion of the Smythe family who was for many years believed to be the grey lady who lurks on the upper floor of the house. Whenever she appears there is a delightful scent of violets, though some think it is a different perfume. Sometimes the aroma will appear without the phantom, when it seems to be stronger than ever and will permeate several rooms at once.

STUDLEY

The little town of Studley was formerly famous for two things: needles and mops. The pitiful ghost who wanders the fields around the town is linked to both.

From 1600 onward the town gradually became a centre for the needle industry. First tens, then scores and finally hundreds of needlemakers lived here. Each was given lengths of steel wire at the start of each week by the merchants who controlled the trade. During the week, the needlemakers would cut the needles to length, pierce an eye at one end and grind the other to a fine point. At the week's end the merchants would again tour the houses to collect the finished pins and pay for the work completed.

Around 1800 the industry began to change. In that year a man named Pardow introduced a steam-driven machine that greatly speeded up the manufacturing process. Instead of paying workers for needles produced in their own homes, Pardow began paying workers for the hours they spent at his machines in his factory. Soon all the needle merchants were using machines.

It was at this time that the mops came into play. For some centuries it had been traditional for agricultural labourers in Warwickshire to be hired on an annual basis by landowners. Each autumn, when the harvest was safely in, the contracts would end. The labourers would then make their way to the hiring fair, held in each of the market towns. There they would seek a position with a landowner, very often the one whose employ they had just left. It was traditional for the male workers to wear in their hats a symbol of their trade: gardeners wore a flower, ploughmen an ear of corn and so forth. The women workers carried a mop, the head of which was likewise decorated with a symbol of their particular skill. As a result these hiring fairs went by the name of Mop Fairs.

At Studley the workers in the new needle factories at first continued the old agricultural tradition. Each autumn they attended the Mop Fair carrying hats or mops adorned with needles, and so found employment. After a while the Mop Fair of Studley became little more than an excuse for merrymaking and feasting. Though in the 1830s it was still a real hiring fair at which the needle merchants hired their factory hands.

The crime that led to the haunting was committed by one of these needle merchants. One day he was seen returning home from the Mop Fair in a terrible rage, muttering threats and curses against his wife who, he declared to anybody who would listen to him, was little better than a common harlot. Bursting into his home, the man began a terrible argument. In front of the horrified servants, he tore the baby from his wife's arms and threw it out of the window. The wife raced outside, but her baby was dead. Mad with grief she ran off and was found some hours later floating lifelessly in a pond, apparently as a result of suicide. The man was hanged, the truth of his allegations never having been discovered.

Soon after the tragedy, the distraught phantom of the woman began to be seen in the house and wandering the fields around the town. The house was later demolished and the ghost does not seem to bother the site any longer. It continues to be seen from time to time flitting across the open fields. The woman is dressed in a long, pale dress and, weeping and wailing, she runs with agitated steps, then fades from view. A most disturbing phantom.

COUGHTON COURT

The beautiful Coughton Court stands, appropriately enough, just outside the village of Coughton, overlooking the busy A435. Today this is a busy but trouble-free highway running across open farmland. But when Coughton Court was first built, it was anything but.

What is now the A435 was then Ryknild Street, an old Roman road that had become a main thoroughfare of medieval England. At Coughton, Ryknild Street crossed the River Arrow, then plunged into the Forest of Arden. Despite its romantic associations with the works of William Shakespeare, a good Warwickshire lad, the Forest of Arden was dark and dangerous, and altogether a rather forbidding place. Wolves and bears lurked there, as did the more dangerous outlaws and footpads who preyed on unwary travellers.

Beside the road at Coughton was erected a large stone cross. Here travellers would wait until there were enough of them making the journey through the forest to deter all but the most determined attackers. Then, after a prayer at the cross, they would set off.

It was a journey of a more dangerous and desperate kind that led to the haunting of Coughton Court. In the 16th and 17th centuries the house and surrounding estates were home to the Throckmorton family, who had a long history of service to the crown, and of rather less successful treachery. In the

The elegant mansion of Coughton Court where past treachery has led to a modern haunting.

1430s Sir John Throckmorton had been Chamberlain to King Henry VI, but in 1584 Francis Throckmorton was executed for being in treasonous correspondence with Mary Queen of Scots.

In 1605 the Throckmortons again dabbled in treason. Sir Thomas Throckmorton, the then head of the family, was a well known Catholic. Although he did not like the accession to the English throne of the Scottish Protestant, King James I, he was willing to accept it. His son in law, Robert Catesby of Northampton, felt more strongly. He masterminded a plot to destroy King James and most of the Protestant nobility by blowing up the House of Lords with a massive charge of gunpowder. The youthful Princess Elizabeth would then be put on the throne and, at swordpoint, forced to appoint a government of Catholics. Catesby, naturally, would be a leading minister. He fondly believed that the people of England would accept such a coup and would willingly embrace the Catholic religion. He was wrong, of course, but the plot was still very real.

As the date for the meeting in the House of Lords drew nearer, Catesby brought his wife back to her father's house at Coughton, then he left to mastermind the coup. This Gunpowder Plot was doomed to failure. The mercenary Guy Fawkes, hired to explode the mine under the House of Lords, was arrested the night before the act was due. The attack to seize the young princess was thwarted at Coombe Abbey, near Coventry. Catesby went on the run.

At Coughton Court, however, the waiting Throckmortons knew nothing about the disaster overtaking the conspiracy. Young Mrs Catesby paced restlessly up and down in what is now the Tapestry Room. Her father, who was not fully aware of what was going on, became increasingly uneasy. He persuaded his daughter to tell him what young Catesby was up to, then raged at his stupidity. When the sound of pounding horses hooves finally came rattling up Ryknild Street towards Coughton Court, it was not the hoped-for victorious conspirators but the soldiers of King James coming to arrest the Throckmortons and all their servants.

The persecution that followed was brutal, but mercifully short. Catesby was killed trying to escape, Fawkes was executed and all their fellow conspirators died in one way or another. Sir Thomas Throckmorton, his daughter and servants were released once it had become clear they had played no active part in the Gunpowder Plot. However, new laws were passed forbidding Catholics from practising their religion and Catholic priests were banned from England in case they proved to be agents of the Pope intent on starting a new plot against the Protestant king.

Mrs Catesby, the one time Miss Throckmorton, never recovered from the death of her husband and the great strain of waiting. Long after the family had returned to Coughton, she would pace restlessly up and down the Tapestry Room thinking of what might have been. After her death, her ghost returned to continue the anxious pacing. She walks still, usually in the evening. Dressed in a long pink dress of early 17th century cut, the spectre crosses the room, sometimes descending the stairs to walk towards the southern wing of the house.

Quite what the poor lady hopes to achieve is unclear. The man she loved died centuries ago and the religious squabbles that dominated England in those days have long since faded into relative unimportance.

ALCESTER

The town of Alcester stands astride the crossing of two Roman roads and beside the confluence of two rivers. It has always been a busy intersection and a market town of some importance in Warwickshire. There was once a Benedictine abbey here but, like most of medieval and ancient Alcester, it has long gone and only foundations await the archaeological spade.

Indeed, Alcester has been built, rebuilt and redesigned so often that it is sometimes difficult to tell what is truly ancient and what is not. The parish church of St Nicholas is a case in point. In the 13th century a new church was built on the site of an earlier structure that was in imminent danger of falling down and, in any case, was too small for the growing population. In 1729 this church was, in its turn, crumbling. The townsfolk called in the architects Thomas and Edward Woodward and asked for a church in the most modern style. The Woodwards obliged and put up a building resembling an ancient

The church at Alcester dominates the town centre.

Greek temple. By the 1870s the citizens of Alcester had gone off this rather stark construction, but they could not afford another redesign. Instead they got a local builder to clad the Ionic structure in a Gothic façade resembling the old 13th century church.

Through all this rebuilding, demolition and reconstruction there was one feature of the church that remained unchanged and unmoved. It stands there still: the tomb of Sir Fulke Greville. Sir Fulke was murdered in bizarre circumstances at Warwick, where his ghost remains very active, and his body was brought here for burial in the parish church of his birthplace. When Sir Fulke's wraith is not stomping about at Warwick, he seems to come here to contemplate his fate.

This ghost is not seen all that often, but he is an impressive sight when he does appear. Dressed in a dark-coloured suit of beautiful velvet and sporting a wide ruff of snow-white linen, he stands to one side of the church not far from the impressive tomb of himself and his wife. This particular phantom does not move, but simply appears from nowhere to remain standing for a few seconds before fading from view once more.

Rather more mobile is the ghost of Captain Richard Hill who is seen in the street outside the Angel Inn, just down the road from the church. Like Sir Fulke, Captain Hill cuts a striking figure. Wearing a wide-brimmed hat adorned with a colourful feather and wearing a riding coat of fine wool, he stomps down the street in high riding boots. And he laughs. It is not, say witnesses, a particularly nice laugh. It is as if he is mocking or jeering at some invisible person that only he can see.

Captain Hill, a military man, came to Alcester in the autumn of 1693. He dressed well, had a purse full of money and displayed all the manners of a gentleman. He put up at the Angel and was welcomed into local society. For a few days all went well, but one evening Hill attended a ball at the nearby Churchill House. After some dancing and a fair amount of drinking, Hill joined the card games in a separate room. He was caught cheating and flew into a great rage. Drawing his sword, Hill attacked the man who had shown up his trick. Only when several locals piled into the fray was Hill disarmed and thrown out of the house.

The angels that adorn the old inn where mysterious events led to a dramatic haunting.

Two days later the owner of the Angel announced that Hill had gone. Nobody else had seen him leave, which was odd. Stranger still was the fact that a man had galloped into Alcester that night, then left just as quickly. A few days later a circular from the magistrates arrived about a man wanted for rape in Redditch, and the description matched that of Captain Hill. Then a coach came from London carrying news of a substantial reward for a 'Captain Richards' who had murdered a man in a quarrel over the affections of a London actress. Again the description matched the appearance of Captain Hill.

Hill was never seen again, at least not alive. His ghost, however, was spotted several times in the Angel and in the street outside. Gossip in Alcester quickly sprung up that he had been killed at the Angel and his body secreted away somewhere. Perhaps the mysterious rider had brought news of his crimes, leading to his death.

Nobody really knows what happened to Captain Richard Hill – if that was his correct name – and given that all concerned are now dead it is unlikely that we will ever find out. Unless, of course, his laughing, mocking ghost cares to tell.

RAGLEY HALL

Standing just outside Alcester is the beautiful Palladian mansion of Ragley Hall, perhaps the most elegant stately home in the county. It is also one of the most haunted.

The house was built in the 1680s for the Seymour family – who later acquired the title of Earl of Hertford and live here still – by the noted architect Robert

The entrance gates to Ragley Hall where various legends and ghosts come together.

Hooke. Born in 1635, he was educated at Oxford and enjoyed a successful career as a chemist and physicist. He formulated Hooke's Law on the expansion of elastic bodies and was the first man to publish the results of studying animals through a microscope. He then became fascinated by arches and how they worked. Although builders and architects had long had experience of constructing arches that did not fall down, nobody had ever worked out the mathematics of how they functioned. Hooke spent years studying loads, bearings and the then new-fangled concept of gravity before triumphantly announcing his theories and equations that explained how arches, and other architectural features, maintained their equilibrium.

Hooke then abandoned science to take up a new career as an architect. His buildings were noted for their daring use of arches and other features. Ragley Hall is no exception. In 1750 architect James Gibb remodelled the interior in stunning fashion while James Wyatt was hired to add a classical-style portico to the front in 1783. The result is one of the finest houses in England. It is open to the public throughout the summer.

It was during some later building work to the outbuildings in 1833 that an ancient grave was disturbed. There had been nothing above ground to indicate the presence of a burial, and a very rich one at that. The lady had clearly been in her grave for many centuries and was adorned with jewelled rings, brooches and a fine necklace set with rubies. She also carried a short sword strapped to her waist. Who this Saxon noblewoman was and why she was buried here were, and remain, complete mysteries.

Quite clearly, however, she did not like being disturbed. Within days of the body being unearthed, a lady clad in a shimmering gown and bedecked with rich jewellery was seen hovering near the site of the burial. Soon the phantom took to horse, galloping off on a wild ride through the grounds of Ragley Hall. A Christian burial for the bones did nothing to lay the ghost, which, if the Saxon lady had been pagan, might be understandable. This dramatic haunting continued for several years, but has now faded.

More likely to be encountered is the old woman who waits outside the gates of Ragley Hall. This phantom seems to be expecting somebody, or something. She scans passing cars and buses as if seeking a familiar face. The fact that at least one visitor has stopped his vehicle to offer her a lift, only for the apparition to vanish abruptly, would indicate that the clothes of the old lady are not so old fashioned as to appear totally out of place. For some reason locals think that this ghost likes to walk down to the nearby brook to drink the cool waters, though nobody ever seems to have seen her do this.

The final ghost of Ragley Hall is thought to be that of a maid who worked here in the 1770s. At this time the Earl of Hertford had an Italian valet whom he had brought back from his visit to Rome on the Grand Tour of European capitals that young men of wealth then undertook to round off their education. The valet was passionately in love with the girl, but none of the staff were entirely certain whether the girl returned his affections. She was, after all, very pretty and several local farmers of some wealth admired her as well as the handsome, but impoverished, valet. Then the young couple vanished one day and were never seen again.

Not long afterwards, the girl began to be seen again, but would vanish inexplicably if anyone approached her. It was some time before it was realised that the figure was a ghost. It was rapidly assumed that the young maid was dead. Though whether she had died naturally after fleeing with the valet or had been killed by him a jealous rage was never discovered. No body has been found and the valet was never caught. It is a mystery that the ghost has done nothing to solve during her regular walks about the grounds of Ragley Hall.

RED HILL

The little village of Red Hill is well named. It stands on the summit of a steep hill where the main road from Worcester to Stratford upon Avon, the A46, crosses from the valley of the Stour to that of the Arrow. This was once a Roman road heading north-west to the wild lands of the Ordovici tribe.

Right on the summit of the hill is the ancient Stag Inn, which has been here for longer than anyone can remember. Certainly parts of the building date from the 16th century, but it is likely that an inn stood here for many generations before that. By 1650 the Stag doubled up as the local court and gaol. The old door to the cell, studded with ironworks to make it more secure, is preserved in the bar. The actual courthouse and cell have long since been amalgamated into

The Stag Inn stands beside an ancient Roman road at Red Hill.

the pub itself and today encompass a small dining area and the ladies' toilets. It is this area that sees most of the phantom activity.

The ghost is that of an elderly woman, dressed in dark or black clothes. Whether she wears a coat, cloak or long dress is not quite clear as witnesses differ in opinion. However, all agree that she is fairly short and seems to be looking for something. Even those who do not see the ghost will suddenly feel rather uncomfortable. Ladies using the toilets report that they suddenly get the impression that somebody is watching them, which must be somewhat unnerving. Generally, however, the ghostly woman does not cause any upset and certainly does nothing to hinder the enjoyment of the splendid meals and welcoming hospitality of this old inn.

The old prison door that may explain the haunting, preserved at the Stag Inn.

It is thought that the ghostly woman may be linked to one of the executions that took place at the crossroads just east of the Stag. It was here that any criminals sentenced to death at the court were taken to be hanged from a large oak tree. The bodies were left dangling for days to warn any would-be miscreants of the summary and stern nature of Warwickshire justice. The ghost, or one very like her, has been seen here on rare occasions. One story claims that a man was executed here for highway robbery and that his distraught mother sat beneath the fatal tree until the magistrate finally gave her permission to take the body away for a decent burial, only for the woman to die a few days later.

·South Warwickshire·

LITTLE LAWFORD

As colourful characters go, nobody could beat 'One Hand Boughton', Squire of Little Lawford during the reign of King Henry VIII. As a boy, Sir Jack Boughton, to give the gentleman his proper name, had lived through the turbulent Wars of the Roses. He had watched the noble families of England tear themselves to pieces as bloody battle followed bloody battle and execution came after execution. He had seen the gentry follow their lords to battle and witnessed local feuds and grudges paid off with violence and murder.

Through all this the Boughtons of Little Lawford had kept their heads and their lands. By carefully supporting all sides, but never actually committing themselves, the family kept out of harm's way and avoided doing harm to others. Unsurprisingly, young Boughton grew to adulthood intent on staying out of political or dynastic trouble of any kind, but even more grimly determined to hang on to his family lands and privileges come what may.

Wary of strangers and jealous of his rights, Sir Jack Boughton farmed his acres and cared for his tenants. But he travelled to market only when he had to do so, and only in a carriage drawn by six horses and accompanied by armed retainers. He was taking no chances. Nor were his lands left unguarded. All around the edges of his estates, Sir Jack erected markers, bold upright posts that nobody could mistake. Every week he rode around his boundaries to check the markers were intact. The thudding hooves of his great black stallion became well known.

And then a newcomer arrived at neighbouring Church Lawford. Not long after, Sir Jack was out riding through his estates when he saw that one of his markers had been moved. In a furious temper he galloped over and put the marker back in its rightful place. Each week for a month the same thing happened. And then the officers of the law came calling for Squire Boughton. The new neighbour was complaining that the markers had been moved onto his property, that Boughton was seeking to steal land that was not his.

Boughton was angrier than ever, but turned up at court armed with historic deeds. His rival had deeds as well and, more seriously, he was well connected to the new king. The judges delayed and prevaricated. They persuaded the newcomer to offer Boughton cash to withdraw his claim. Boughton refused. In the end, the judges nervously pronounced that the lands belonged to Boughton, but that the squire had been wrong to move the boundary markers without legal sanction. The newcomer vengefully sought the severest sentence available under the harsh laws of the time. Boughton lost his hand to the axe of the public executioner.

The lane running down to Little Lawford's ford where the dramatic ghost of One Hand Boughton has been seen.

Waving the bloody stump at his tormentor, Boughton vowed that the man would never rest easy. Nor did he. Day after day, whenever the business of managing his estates allowed, Boughton would ride his black charger to the disputed lands and wave his disfigured arm at his rival. If the two men met in village or town, Boughton would taunt and jeer. Soon the man left the area, leaving Boughton to farm his acres unchallenged once again.

Even death could not stop One Hand Boughton from the enjoyment of his family lands. No sooner had the good folk of Little Lawford buried their squire, than he returned in spectral form. Mounted on his great charger, One Hand Boughton galloped the countryside, scaring the wits out of the farmhands and villagers who encountered him. He rode the lanes in his fine black carriage pulled by six black horses. And he stomped about his former home at Lawford Hall, appearing most often in his old bedroom and the upstairs corridor.

After two centuries of ghostly activity by their colourful ancestor, the Boughtons had had enough. In the 1730s Sir Edward Boughton decided on an exorcism. The local vicar did not feel up to the task, so he sent for wise old Parson Hall of Great Harborough. Having visited the scene of the haunting, Parson Hall decided that no less than twelve clergy would be needed to lay a spirit as formidable as that of One Hand Boughton. It was later whispered that four of the clergymen who assembled on the appointed day were bishops come to learn from old Parson Hall.

Be that as it may, Hall arranged that each clergyman should hold a lighted candle. The man was to continue to recite the appropriate words as long as his candle burned, but was to cease if it went out. They gathered in the haunted bedroom and began the ceremony. Almost at once one of the candles went out, and the vicar holding it fell silent. One Hand Boughton was about. One by one the candles went out as the clergy pitted themselves against the long dead squire.

Finally the only candle left casting shadows around the dark room was that held by Parson Hall. Instead of continuing with the exorcism, Hall broke off and began talking directly to One Hand. The vicar and the ghost did a deal. Boughton would allow himself to be confined in a green glass bottle, on condition that the bottle was kept on his acres and that he was free to roam his lands for two hours every night. The agreement was made, the ghost entered the bottle and wise old Parson Hall inserted a stopper then threw it into a pond.

And so things went on. Peace returned to Lawford Hall, though the powerful spirit of One Hand Boughton rode the fields around the hour of midnight. When the main road south of the village became a turnpike, a toll gate was erected and a keeper installed to collect fees from every vehicle that used the road. Every vehicle but one, that is, for One Hand Boughton and his great coach were exempt. It is said that a temporary toll keeper was found a gibbering wreck one morning. He had tried to stop the phantom coach and had been overwhelmed by the anger of Squire Boughton. It was days before he recovered enough to tell his story, and he insisted the company move him to a different area.

In 1780 tragedy came to Little Lawford when Sir Theodosius Boughton was murdered by his brother-in-law, who was plotting to take over the estates. There being no direct heir, the family titles and lands passed to the Leigh family, and the name Boughton-Leigh was adopted. Ten years later Sir John Boughton-Leigh decided to abandon the old Lawford Hall with its memories of murder and its active ghost. He moved the family to his property just north of Rugby. Which is the scene of another haunting.

RUGBY

Just north of the town centre of Rugby the modern dual carriageway of the A426 follows a route through industrial estates, bypassing completely the old Leicester Road with its houses and the grand edifice of Brownsover Hall. This monumental pile was erected in 1857 by the famous architect Sir George Gilbert Scott on the orders of Sir John Ward Boughton-Leigh.

The Leighs acquired their double-barrelled name when they inherited the much haunted Boughton estates of nearby Little Lawford. But if they thought a new house at Rugby would put an end to the ghostly manifestations of One Hand Boughton, they reckoned without the determination of that colourful Tudor squire. Only a few days after Sir John moved into his grand new home, the ghost came calling.

A footman heard a carriage approaching the house up the sweeping drive from what was then the main road to Leicester. Thinking some late night guest was arriving, the man roused a maid and opened the front door. He was startled to be confronted by the towering figure of the ghostly one-armed squire, apparently surveying with some satisfaction the new home of his descendants. Several times since then the phantom coach has been seen driving from Little Lawford down the lanes and over to Rugby. Strangely, it has not been seen returning. But return it must for One Hand Boughton is a very active ghost on the wide acres that were once his.

But Brownsover Hall has its own ghosts. Ironically one of them is the Sir John who moved the family to the new home. He haunts the old billiard room, today used as a bar now that the Hall is a luxurious and welcoming hotel. Dressed in casual country clothes as befits a landed Victorian squire, Sir John strolls nonchalantly through the room ignoring any mere mortals he may meet. There is also a lady dressed in Victorian fashion who walks down the staircase, past the grand fireplace and out into the grounds. Nobody is quite clear who she is, though it must be presumed she is one of the Boughton-Leigh ladies who lived here in Victorian times.

The main fireplace at Brownsover Hall, now a hotel, where the grey lady is often seen.

PRINCETHORPE

The ghosts of Princethorpe are an enigmatic bunch. There are local legends in plenty to explain them, but no recorded history. The ghosts themselves rarely appear together, though one man claimed to see them involved in a scene of violence and murder. The most active is a phantom priest. Dressed in a long black cassock, the man walks gently among the woods west of the village, bothering nobody. Seen less often, although rather more dramatic, is the ghostly nun. She runs as if upset or angry about something. Like the priest, she frequents the woods but she has occasionally appeared in nearby fields as well. The most exciting ghosts are those that are seen least often. A troop of armed men wearing helmets and breastplates marches up from the village to the same woods where the other ghosts roam.

Local legend has it that the ghosts date from the days of Queen Elizabeth I, when the Pope and the Catholic King of Spain intrigued endlessly to oust the Protestant Elizabeth and replace her with a reliably Catholic monarch. The mighty Spanish Armada was the most open and violent attempt, but there were frequent plots to murder the Queen or to foment rebellion. Fanatical Catholics, usually priests recruited from English families, were sent to England to arrange the plots.

The hapless Catholics of England, the vast majority of whom far preferred an English Protestant on the throne to a foreign Catholic, were caught in the middle. Their religion might be tolerated and they were free to conduct services in private, but their priests were suspected of treachery and hounded by the government.

It seems that a Catholic priest from abroad came to Warwickshire to minister to the spiritual needs of the local Catholics. He sanctified marriages, conducted baptisms and performed funeral rights for those who had died since a priest last came that way. Of course, he had to stay out of sight of officialdom, so he holed up in the woods. A loyal former nun, now living as a layperson in Princethorpe, brought him food supplies and directed him to wherever his services were needed.

The college at Princethorpe, near which the village ghosts have appeared.

But the government came to hear of the priest roaming Warwickshire and, fearful that he was a religious fanatic planning what we would now call a terrorist outrage, sent armed men to arrest him. The nun managed to warn the priest of the approaching force, but the soldiers overtook the pair. In the ensuing struggle the nun was killed, while the priest made his escape. He fled abroad, never to return except in spectral form.

The local Catholic community, however, survived. In the 19th century an order of French nuns opened a house in Princethorpe. It is now a Catholic school of fine reputation and impressive buildings.

ROYAL LEAMINGTON SPA

Royal Leamington Spa was once just plain Leamington. It was an unremarkable little village for centuries, distinguished only by the fact that the mineral waters of the nearby spring were said to have medicinal properties.

In 1786, however, the local doctor William Abbots built a small bathing pool to hold the mineral waters and announced that Leamington was a spa. Taking the waters was then a hugely fashionable thing to do, and the families of quality who flocked to spa towns brought much wealth and prosperity with them. Bath and Matlock were already fine towns, and now it was the turn of Leamington Spa, which gained its royal prefix on the instructions of Queen Victoria, who came here in 1838 when the health boom was at its height. The fine buildings and elegant architecture that dominate the town date from this period.

Of the ghosts, only one dates from Leamington's days of glory. In 1820 an elderly lady who had come to Leamington to take the water was murdered by her maid. The killer pocketed her victim's impressively valuable collection of jewels and fled out along the road towards Kenilworth. Unfortunately for her, the body was discovered before she could get clean away. Mounted men overtook her at Chesford Bridge over the River Avon and dragged her back to face stern justice in the shape of a hangman's noose. It is her ghost that runs out of Leamington on the Kenilworth road, now the A452.

Rather less dramatic is the story behind the haunting that affected the Jack and Jill pub on Newlands Road in the 1980s. The former landlord, Graham Boulton, had been a long serving and hugely popular host when he died still in harness. His ghost was seen several times around the pub, always seeming to be checking that things were as they should be. He has not been seen recently. Perhaps the phantom has moved on, having reassured himself that his beloved pub passed into capable hands.

Likewise rarely seen these days is the lady in grey who once roamed so frequently around the Manor House Hotel. She was thought to be a housekeeper who, like Mr Boulton, could not bear to be parted from her beloved job.

SHUCKBURGH

The A425 east of Southam looks much like any other stretch of main road in Warwickshire. But there must be something odd about the place for it has seen far more than its fair share of violence, murder and ghosts.

First on the scene was one Lieutenant Sharp of the militia. He seems to have served bravely in the war against Napoleon's plans for a united European Empire organised on the model of the French state. However, when the war ended Lt Sharp did not do well. He joined the local militia, a part-time military force organised to defend the country against invasion, perhaps to rekindle some of his military spirit, but he remained morose and unpopular. Whatever the problems that Lt Sharp had, they were enough for Sir Stewkley Shuckburgh of Shuckburgh Hall to object when Lt Sharp came calling for his daughter, Lucy.

Lt Sharp persisted, however, and a definite romance was soon blossoming. Sir Stewkley was no more impressed by his daughter's suitor on close acquaintance than he had been to start with. Rising to the full heights of which a Georgian squire was capable, Sir Stewkley banned Lt Sharp from the house and informed Lucy that she must never see the young man again. She protested and objected, but Sir Stewkley was adamant. Finally, however, he agreed that his daughter could see her lover one last time to say her goodbyes.

Lt Sharp called and the young couple walked out along the road towards Napton on the Hill where they had enjoyed many happy hours. Then tragedy struck. Lt Sharp drew a pistol and blew out the brains of young Lucy. He then turned the gun on himself and soon both lay dead in the dusty road, where their bodies were discovered by the servants sent out by Sir Stewkley to find out why his daughter had not returned by the agreed time.

After his dashing and exciting life in the cavalry, the tragic Lieutenant Sharp of Shuckburgh found peacetime life very dull.

The lovers have returned many times since. Shuckburgh Hall is still a private house, but they have been seen out on the road as well as at Lucy's old home. The ghosts give no hint of the tragedy that befell them. They walk slowly as if lost in their own world where love can conquer all, but so sadly led only to death.

The second murder occurred a few years later, in 1820. A farmer from Upper Shuckburgh travelled to market in Southam to sell his produce. He did not return that evening, and his wife assumed he had stayed over in town for some reason. Next morning she opened her door to find, not her husband but a neighbour named Smith. This Smith told her that he had just met her husband's ghost in the main road. The ghost, Smith said, bore the marks of stab wounds and had named another neighbour, Peter Thomas, as the murderer.

The shocked wife sent out friends and soon enough the farmer's body was found bundled into a ditch beside the road with stab wounds, just as Smith had said. Thomas was promptly arrested and, when he could produce no alibi, was sent to trial in Warwick. The case puzzled the locals for Thomas was a respectable man who had no grudge against the victim and had no possible motive for the killing.

When the case came before Lord Chief Justice Raymond, he ruled that the evidence given by the ghost was hearsay and, therefore, inadmissible in court unless the ghost appeared in person. As is usual when a witness needs to be found, legal papers were sent out throughout Warwickshire demanding the presence of the ghost of the murdered man at court on a stated day. The ghost did not appear, but legal history had been made.

Thomas was acquitted as there was no other evidence against him. There was, however, a growing body of evidence that Smith had had a serious argument with the dead man at market. Had he committed the crime and invented the ghost story to divert attention onto Thomas? Or was his sighting of a ghost with a message entirely true? We will never know.

NAPTON ON THE HILL

If any village in England deserves its name, it is Napton on the Hill. The village tumbles down the side of the tall, steep hill that makes this one of the most windswept in the county. Right on the summit of the hill, standing alone among open fields some distance from the nearest houses, is the ancient church of St Lawrence. Much of the structure dates from a 13th century rebuilding, though earlier remnants and more recent additions are also to be found. It is a charming church with much to offer the casual visitor, but in many ways it is an odd one as well.

When the good folk of Napton were converted to the Christian faith, they at first worshipped beside a cross set up in the village street. Some generations later it was decided that a proper church was needed. Good building stone was sent for and an experienced builder hired to supervise the locals in their work. The villagers set to with a will, erecting the church at the bottom of the village. They were amazed to find that on the first Sunday after they had begun the construction, all the stones and tools had been moved overnight to the top of the hill. Who had done the deed was unknown. The villagers laboriously moved everything back down the hill and began building afresh. Next Sunday the same thing happened. Concluding that the fairies or little people had good reason for wanting the church on top of the hill, the villagers proceeded to erect their new place of worship on its current, rather isolated location.

Napton folk had some odd funeral habits until fairly recently. A corpse had to be kept in the family house until the funeral, after which it was carried out feet first and the door left open until after the burial. Nor could a body be buried on Sunday, and it must not remain unburied beyond Saturday night. If any of these conditions were not met, it was firmly believed, the dead would return to take two more members of their family to join them in death.

The path leading to the church at Napton on the Hill where one of the local ghosts is most likely to be met.

With such an odd background, the ghosts of Napton on the Hill are almost mundane. The first is an elderly lady who walks up from the village towards the church. She is dressed in black, wears a close-fitting bonnet and carries an umbrella. This particular ghost is not much bother to anyone. She simply strolls up to the church from time to time, no doubt revisiting the path she took in life on her way to worship and, perhaps, the route taken by her corpse when it came to be her turn to be buried before Saturday night.

Altogether different are the two ghosts that appear in the church itself. These two ladies date from a much earlier period, being dressed in the stiff, full-skirted fashions of the 16th century. Nobody knows who these two middle-aged ladies might be, but they are generally reckoned to be a bad omen. They appear in the front pew as if attending a service, either deep in prayer or apparently listening intently to a sermon. They may be seen several times in a few days, then be absent for years on end.

But whenever the two Tudor ladies do appear, local folk brace themselves for unwelcome news.

HARBURY

The bustling village of Harbury might appear to be an unremarkable and inoffensive sort of a place. There are some shops and a church, and enough houses to provide customers for both.

In years gone by, this was one of those places in Warwickshire where 'Thomasing' was a popular activity. At 6 am on 21 December, St Thomas's Day, the church bells would be rung. Then the poor folk of the village would carry a box from door to door singing:

> Little Cock Robin sat on a wall,
> We wish you a merry Christmas
> And a great snowfall;
> Apples to eat
> And nuts to crack
> We wish you a merry Christmas
> With a rap, tap, tap.

The householders would then donate whatever spare food they could to help the poorer families through the winter.

It was those same church bells that, on a fateful day in the 1820s, signalled the start of the haunting of Harbury. A Sunday morning service was heralded by the ringing of the bells and was made special by the christening of various Harbury infants. One of the men whose child was being baptised was an

A tragic ghost of a woman carrying a baby walks the streets of Harbury.

evil-tempered farm labourer who was generally shunned by those unwilling to get involved in a pointless argument. On his way home from the service, the man suddenly murdered his wife and baby. There could be no doubt about his guilt, but he remained totally silent throughout his short imprisonment and brief trial. The man went to the gallows without asking for mercy, nor explaining his actions.

The ghost of the poor woman, carrying a young baby wrapped in a shawl in her arms, has been seen leaving the church and walking through the streets of Harbury. She is recreating her last, fatal journey and vanishes at the spot where she was killed.

LIGHTHORNE

As the armies of the King and of Parliament formed up for battle at Edgehill, a few miles to the south, the good folk of Lighthorne shut their doors and hid their goods from the notoriously light-fingered soldiers that marched and countermarched across the landscape. One man,

The lane leading to the church at Lighthorne where a woman who died of grief is seen.

however, chose to set off to join the fighting. Burning with religious zeal for the Puritan form of Christianity and appalled by the King's high-handed imposition of high church rituals, the young man set off to fight for Parliament.

He never came back, being killed on the field of battle.

When the news was brought to his wife, a bride of less than three months, she collapsed in the street. She never really recovered from the shock, wasting away and dying just a few months later. Her ghost returns to Church Lane, where she heard the terrible news, and appears as a thin, pale young woman with drawn features and a tear-stained face. Sometimes she seems just to stand and stare, but at other times she weeps and wails in mourning for her lost love. She can be a heartbreaking ghost to encounter.

The second ghost at Lighthorne is also linked to tragedy, this time to a brutal murder. Sometime in the early Victorian period a farm girl was working in a field off the lane leading to Moreton Morrell. She was murdered here, her head being beaten in by some frenzied maniac. Nobody was ever caught for the crime, which may explain why the girl returns time and again to the lane. She is accompanied by a strange feeling of threat or fear that at least one witness found to be absolutely overwhelming.

BURTON DASSETT

The little village of Burton Dassett entered history briefly in 1642 during the Civil War. A young Roundhead cavalry officer by the name of Oliver Cromwell led his regiment into the place. Excited scouts met him here with tales of a vast Royalist army nearby, but the reports were rather garbled and contradictory. Cromwell leapt from his horse and ran up the stairs to the top of the church tower. From there he was able to see the King's army as it marched across distant fields and to count its numbers accurately. He then reported back to his superiors, enabling them to position the Parliamentary army in time for what became the Battle of Edgehill. At the time, Cromwell was a relatively unknown young man out of East Anglia, but his prompt action that day at Burton Dassett brought him to the attention of the Parliamentarian high command and put him on the road to greatness.

The ghost of Burton Dassett is to be encountered in the fields outside the village proper. She goes by the name of Jenny, though nobody seems very clear who she was or when she lived. This Jenny is a cruel girl who seems to have a grudge against humanity, or at least that part of it that visits Burton Dassett. She carries a lantern giving out a clear blue and yellow light, which she waves to

The hills outside Burton Dassett where a mischievous spirit seeks to mislead travellers.

attract attention. She then beckons as if wanting people to follow her. Thinking the young lady may be in trouble of some kind, kind-hearted folk may be tempted to follow. But they should ignore her. Jenny delights in leading people into marshes and ditches and over steep banks.

Such are the pranks of Burton Dassett's Jenny. These days most people travel by car, so the bobbing lantern of the ghost is less obvious than it was in the days when people walked or rode the dark lanes at night without the advantage of blazing headlights. Whether this is why Jenny has not been seen much in recent years is unclear. Perhaps she lurks there just as she always did, waiting for some fool who does not know her to set off across the fields in pursuit of the dancing blue and yellow lantern.

EDGEHILL

Until October 1642, Edgehill was just another hill in Warwickshire. Then war came to the windswept slopes and things were never the same again.

Arguments had been simmering throughout England for years. King Charles I felt that he had been appointed by God to rule the country and care for its people. He chose to plunge England into unnecessary wars, that he then lost, and to move the Church of England more towards Catholic doctrine. Both were unpopular policies, made worse by Charles's habit of raising taxes without asking the approval of Parliament, by this date accepted as expressing the views of the nobility and gentry – who by and large were the ones who paid the taxes.

In 1640 Charles at last summoned a Parliament to ask for more taxes to be raised. The Parliament met in tumult, demanding an end to Charles's incompetent dictatorial rule. When Charles seemed intent on continuing just as before, Parliament asked to be able to dismiss the king's ministers and to have control of the armed forces, neither of which the king would allow. After two years of wrangling, Charles left London for Nottingham. He raised the royal standard and sent out messages throughout the kingdom asking all loyal men to rally to his flag and take up arms against what he viewed as a rebellious

Parliament. In its turn, Parliament sent out messages urging all loyal men to rally to their flag against a king who had broken the laws of the land and ignored the constitution. War broke out.

The first moves by both sides were expeditions to take control of the various arsenals and treasuries that were scattered across the kingdom. On 22 October both armies happened to be in Warwickshire on their different missions. Cavalry scouts spotted each other, though only the

The battlefield of Edgehill. The Royal Army began the day on top of the hill, then advanced down towards the foreground.

Parliamentarians had a good idea of the enemy's strength. The king, uncertain of the army facing him, took position on Edgehill. The towering hill allowed him to dominate the surrounding countryside from a position of strength.

Arriving on the scene next day, the Parliamentary commander, the Earl of Essex, did not fall into the trap of attacking this strong position, but instead opened up with his artillery. After suffering some casualties, the king decided to attack. Led by the king's nephew, the experienced Prince Rupert, the Royalist cavalry surged down the hill and swept away the Parliamentarian horse. The infantry moved more slowly, reaching the Parliamentarian position as the cavalry rode out of sight. The fighting was long and hard, ending only as night fell. The victory had been won by the king.

Rupert and other professional soldiers urged the king to advance rapidly on London. Charles refused, stating he had beaten the enemy, and instead opened negotiations with Parliament. The talks got nowhere and the war was to drag on for years until Parliament won and King Charles was executed in Whitehall.

While the fighting raged back and forth across England, strange things were happening at Edgehill. On Christmas Eve local villagers were startled to see two large armies gathering for battle again on the old battlefield. No soldier had

The charge of the Royalist cavalry at Edgehill swept all before it, and left a supernatural legacy at the site.

been seen in the area for some weeks and the weather was unsuitable for campaigning, which involved men sleeping in the open air. As before, the battle opened with artillery fire followed by a cavalry charge. But then the armies abruptly vanished. They had been phantom troops. The ghostly armies marched again several times in the following weeks.

At his headquarters in Oxford, King Charles heard the stories of marching ghost armies and sent six gentlemen to investigate. They interviewed the people who had seen the ghosts and were preparing to write up their report when a sudden clamour alerted them to the fact that the ghosts were marching again. The gentlemen hurried to ride to the battlefield and saw the ghosts for themselves. One man recognised a friend who had died in the fighting: Sir Edmund Verney.

Verney had been one of the most prominent casualties of the battle. He was a noted opponent of the king's policies but, as the official bearer of the royal standard, had felt it his duty to ride with his monarch. During the battle, Verney had been surrounded by enemy soldiers who demanded he hand over the flag. 'My life is my own,' replied Verney, 'but this standard is the King's and I cannot surrender it.' They killed him, but even then could not prise his fingers from the flagpole, so they hacked off his arm. A Royalist counter-attack recaptured the flag and it was returned to the king, still with Verney's severed hand gripping it tight. The hand was returned to Verney's home for burial but his body was never identified among the thousands that littered the field.

Several times over the following months the spectral battle was played out on the fields around Edgehill, witnessed by hundreds of reliable people. Gradually, however, the ghostly re-enactment was fought less and less frequently until by about 50 years after the battle it was seen no more.

But some ghosts remain. One is a tall, dashing man mounted on a white horse who gallops down the slope waving his sword over his head in martial valour. Inevitably the ghost is identified as being Prince Rupert, the courageous commander who led the Royalist cavalry to victory. More likely, perhaps, this is the ghost of some nameless man who died that terrible day.

Another phantom is that of a shorter, dark haired man who seems to be searching for something. He walks slowly, scanning the ground but never finding what it is he seeks. Perhaps this is Sir Edmund Verney searching in vain for his lost hand.

CHARLECOTE PARK

Charlecote Park is best known outside of Warwickshire for a fairly petty crime that was to have great consequences. In 1585 the owner, Sir Thomas Lucy, caught a young man from nearby Stratford upon Avon red-handed, poaching deer from the estate. Indeed, the man was selling the butchered joints to the landlord of the Dun Cow Inn at Wilmcote when arrested. Before the man could be brought to trial, however, he had penned a few lines of verse and nailed them to the gates of Charlecote Park. Then he fled to London.

The verse ran:

> *A Parliament member, a Justice of the Peace,*
> *At home a poor scarecrow, in London an ass;*
> *If lousy is Lucy, as some folk miscall it,*
> *Then Lucy is lousy, whatever befall it.*
> *He thinks himself great*
> *Yet an ass in his state*

We allow by his ears
With but asses to mate.
Sir Thomas was too covetous
To cover so much deer;
When horns enough upon his head
Most plainly did appear.
Had not his worship one deer left,
What then, he had a wife
Took pains enough to find him horns
Should hold him during life.

No doubt the verse would soon have been forgotten were it not for the fact that the young man on the run was William Shakespeare, who found lasting fame as poet and playwright in London. He is believed to have caricatured Sir Thomas Lucy as Mr Justice Shallow in the plays *Henry IV Part 2* and *The Merry Wives of Windsor*.

Charlecote Park.

The lake at Charlecote Park, where two separate ghosts are seen.

Within Warwickshire, however, Charlecote Park is best known as being a haunt of witches. They are said to gather here from all over the county on various nights of the full moon to indulge in whatever rituals it is that witches undertake.

Whether the ghosts of Charlecote have anything to do with Shakespeare or witches is unclear. The more active of the phantoms is that of a young lady who walks quietly and soulfully beside the lake in the grounds of the house. She is generally thought to be the ghost of a servant who committed suicide by drowning herself in the lake, though what prompted her to take such a dreadful step is not known.

Seen less often is the shade of a Sir Thomas Lucy who was murdered here in 1262 by two of his servants. They dragged the body down to the lake from the house, then a much earlier structure, and threw it into the waters. It lay undiscovered long enough for the villainous pair to make their escape. The ghostly Sir Thomas walks from the house to the lake with slow, measured tread. Perhaps he was not quite dead when dumped in the chill, dark waters and his ghost recreates his final journey.

STRATFORD UPON AVON

The most famous resident of Stratford, past or present, is William Shakespeare. The bard was born here, the son of a glovemaker. Having got into trouble poaching deer, he ran off to London, returning home only after gaining fame and fortune.

The house in Henley Street where his father lived and worked and, it is presumed, where Shakespeare was born is now a museum dedicated to the great man. For a great many years the property was haunted by a kindly old lady. She would potter about, walking quietly through doors and looking out of windows. Many visitors mistook her for a member of staff and were most surprised when she abruptly vanished if they tried to talk to her. For whatever reason, she has not been seen since the 1950s.

South of the town centre lies Ettington Park, perhaps the finest example of Victorian stately home design in England. It was built for the Shirley family who had owned the lands since the 11th century, but is now a hotel.

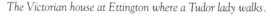

The Victorian house at Ettington where a Tudor lady walks.

Despite the fact that the current building dates back only to 1858, it is haunted by a ghost from the previous house. The lady seems to date from Tudor times, judging by the dress that she wears. When the old house was standing she was seen most often on or near the staircase and was generally thought to have been the wraith of a servant who died after falling down the grand sweep of steps. Since the rebuilding, she is likely to be seen almost anywhere on the premises.

ATHERSTONE ON STOUR

The main road from Stratford upon Avon to Oxford runs just outside the charming little village of Atherstone on Stour, along the Stour valley and past Alderminster. Many years ago a farmer from Atherstone was drinking at Alderminster. He was exceedingly proud of a new horse he had bought and laid a bet with his drinking companions about how fast he could ride home.

Off he rode at high speed, but he was doomed never to reach his farm. As he turned off the main road into the lane leading down to Atherstone itself his horse went under a tree. In the darkness of the night the rider failed to notice a low-hanging branch, and this struck him on the head, killing him instantly. On dark, moonless nights the man's ghost recreates the fatal ride. A local tradition claims that any person who sees the ghost once will see it twice more before their own death.

The fatal road junction at Atherstone on Stour where a ghost recreates an accident of long ago.

PRESTON ON STOUR

The phantom of Preston on Stour is best avoided. Anyone who sees a strange, unearthly glow in the lanes or fields hereabouts would be well advised to flee at high speed before the apparition takes more solid form.

This is the Dun Cow, a fabled phantom creature that dominates the folklore of Warwickshire, but which becomes terrifying reality in the dusk around Preston. Many centuries ago a famine struck the county, and the people faced slow death from starvation. To their aid came the Dun Cow. Where the creature originated, nobody was ever entirely certain though it was generally thought that it was a fairy creature. One day it ambled into a village looking sleek, fat and healthy, quite unlike the starving animals of the locality.

Cautiously, the villagers approached the cow, which stood taller than any they had ever seen. The udders of the beast were plump and filled with milk. As

The centre of Preston on Stour was the scene for a supernatural encounter that has left its terrifying mark on the area.

the cow made no objection, the first villager brought a bucket and soon had it filled with foaming, creamy milk. With this he fed his children. Soon all the villagers were lining up with buckets. The Dun Cow stood patiently while everyone had a turn. When each villager had filled a bucket, the cow ambled off to the next village.

And so the Dun Cow toured Warwickshire, bringing relief from the famine. No matter how many people approached it, the cow allowed each to fill one bucket – but no more. And no matter how many buckets were filled the amazing beast seemed to have as much milk left as ever.

But then an unscrupulous old woman from Preston had an idea. She noticed that the Dun Cow gave an endless supply of milk, but that each person was allowed only one bucketful. She set to work and constructed a bucket that, although it appeared ordinary enough, had a sieve at the bottom that led to a pipe connected to a vast vat. By milking the Dun Cow into the sieve, the old woman reasoned, she could extract far more than her fair share.

The next time the Dun Cow wandered into Preston, the old lady put her plan into action. The cow suspected nothing, allowing the woman to approach with her bucket and start milking. As the minutes passed, the animal stood patiently while the woman milked. But as the minutes became hours, the Dun Cow grew restless. Then it grew angry. Realising it had been tricked, it turned furiously on the old lady and attacked. The beast gored her to death, then charged at the other folk of Preston and their houses. Having laid waste the village and demolished the houses with supernatural strength, the cow lifted its tail and raced off.

The Dun Cow gave its milk no more, but it had not gone entirely. It returns in phantom form from time to time. But the ghostly Dun Cow is angry and vengeful. It attacks anyone it meets, smashing fences, destroying hedges and flattening buildings.

This was a peaceful, generous creature sent by the fairy folk that was driven to anger by the wickedness and greed of humanity. And now it returns from time to time to wreak revenge on the human race that betrayed it.

The tale of the Dun Cow is also associated with Dunsmore Heath, to the south-west of Rugby.

MEON HILL

The landscape of south-western Warwickshire is generally flat, with just a gentle rise and fall of the landscape to add interest. But near the village of Mickleton the imposing bulk of Meon Hill dominates the skyline. This is the northern outlier of the Cotswolds, which run south-west into Gloucestershire and beyond.

This has long been a hill of legend and mystery. A labourer working on its slopes in the 16th century is rumoured to have unearthed a pot filled with ancient gold coins. The hill itself is said to have been created by the Devil, who threw a huge mound of earth at Evesham Abbey, so angry was he at the sanctity of the monks there. Timely prayers by the monks caused the missile to swerve in flight and land near Mickleton instead.

The heights of Meon Hill dominate the south-west of Warwickshire,
both physically and in tales of horror.

In 1945 Meon Hill leapt to national attention. A gruesome murder took place there that, for a while, pushed news of the war against Hitler's Germany off the front pages of the newspapers. Charles Walton was a local farm labourer aged 72 who was known to have an uncanny knack of communicating with horses, cattle and other creatures. He kept toads as pets and spoke to the birds in the hedgerows.

On 14 February he went out to re-lay hedgerows on Meon Hill, but never returned. His niece, Edith, found him next day. He was lying spread-eagled on his

*The Devil himself lurks on Meon Hill
to trap the unwary.*

back with a pitchfork pinning him to the ground through the throat. He had been almost disembowelled by the billhook he had been using, the deep cuts being in the shape of a cross.

The local police sent for Superintendent Robert Fabian of Scotland Yard, a detective famous for solving unusual cases. Fabian found that the villagers would not talk to him and offered no explanation. He did discover, however, that one local farmer was suffering from blighted crops and sick livestock while his neighbours were doing well. Moreover, carving a cross on the body was said to be a traditional Warwickshire method of ensuring a witch stayed dead. Fabian came to believe that the farmer had murdered Walton in the belief he was a witch responsible for the poor crops. Understandably, Fabian hesitated to take the case to court without firm evidence and, since there was none, the murder went unavenged.

All of which pales into insignificance beside the belief among Warwickshire peasants for centuries that Meon Hill was a gateway to Hell itself. Numerous legends and stories grew up about the activities of the Evil One and his presence on the hill. Most agree on two key features. The first is that when the gates of Hell are open a large, savage dog with shaggy black fur roams the hill. The hound patrols the slopes to keep mortals away from the entrance to the underworld. Those who see the dog are well advised to flee the hill as fast as possible for certain death awaits those who push on. The second generally agreed fact is that the Devil comes out of Meon Hill mounted on a great black charger and accompanied by a pack of hell hounds. With these he sets off to hunt down the souls of the damned, dragging them back to Hell through the gates of Meon Hill.

The deaths of notorious criminals or wicked characters across Warwickshire are said to have been accompanied by the call of a hunting horn from somewhere on Meon Hill, followed by the sounds of baying hounds echoing through the night.

The hill may appear to be a pleasant spot, and the prehistoric earthworks that crown its summit are of great archaeological interest. But this is probably not an area in which to linger for too long.

ILMINGTON

The parish church at Ilmington is exactly as an English country church should be. It is well cared for and its ancient stone walls blend into the scenery as if it has always stood there. It has over its door the coat of arms of the de Montfort Earls of Warwick and within its walls the tombs of its medieval vicars and more recent parishioners, be they grand or humble. In the 1930s the church was adorned with new woodwork by the highly regarded Robert Thomson of Kilburn in North Yorkshire, who famously added a small mouse to all his works.

An intriguing ghost lurks in and around these ancient walls. The phantom is of a man dressed smartly in a long riding coat of old fashioned cut. He is seen quite distinctly and, although he appears solid and real, there is something odd about him that attracts attention. Perhaps it is his out-dated suit, perhaps his distracted behaviour or maybe he just looks odd. This ghost is thought to be that of one Edward Golding who was the parish clerk some 250 years ago. He obviously loved the church, for he has never left. Strangely, his tomb carries the epitaph 'His performance of the duties of his office fell far short of their obligations and importance'. The words were carved at his own instruction, though it is doubtful if anyone else in the parish shared his views.

Altogether more sinister is the Night Coach, a fearsome apparition that haunts the lane and byways crossing the hills above the village. It favours the rutted byway of Pig Lane, which runs past an ancient earthwork. This mysterious structure has never been excavated, so it is

Ilmington church has numerous reminders of its past – including a ghost.

impossible to date it accurately. The terrifying coach hurtles at high speed across the countryside, oblivious to walls, fences, trees and still more to humans. It is a large black contraption pulled by six jet-black horses. Some say the coachman is headless, others that there is no driver at all. Some say the coach is empty and dark, others that it is filled with the souls of the damned. All agree that it moves in total and eerie silence.

It is also agreed that the Night Coach is an evil vehicle. The few people who have witnessed it in recent years were wise enough to dive for cover to avoid being seen. Nobody knows where this fearsome apparition comes from or where it goes. But it is best not to take any chances.

HONINGTON

Warwickshire is a county of witches and there are numerous tales of witchcraft, many dating back centuries. As recently as 1875 a woman was forcibly 'pricked' – an ancient custom involving sticking a pin into the flesh to see if the woman bleeds, for if she does not she is a confirmed witch.

Only at Honington, however, does a witch appear in phantom and benevolent guise. This is Betty, a famously skilful lady when it came to mixing

The ghostly witch of Honington is seen often on this bridge just outside the village.

healing potions and the like in the early 18th century. She sought out herbs, roots and berries in the countryside around Honington at all seasons and in all weathers, with her pipe clamped firmly between her teeth. After her death, old Betty returned in spectral form. She sits on a wall just outside the village, nodding jovially at passers-by. What her mission might be, or if she has one, is a total mystery.

BRAILES

George Fox lived an entirely straightforward life up until the age of nineteen. He had grown up in a village in Leicestershire, then been apprenticed to a cobbler in Nottingham to learn a trade. But one day he suddenly got up, walked out of his workshop and never came back.

For some years Fox wandered England in search of religious truth and sanctity. He found it in neither the established Church of England nor in any of the various non-conformist sects. He gradually came to the conclusion that the only true path to religious peace was to have God in your heart and to live your life according to the wishes of God. In 1647, at the age of 23, Fox began to preach this new doctrine to anyone who would listen to him.

He quickly won a circle of admirers, which he dubbed the Society of Friends. Fox's religious conviction was such that he simply could not stay silent in the face of what he believed to be error. In 1649 he interrupted a vicar preaching a sermon in Nottingham, getting involved in an undignified fight in the church and ending up in prison. The following year a similar incident saw him brought to court in Derby. Asked if he had anything to say before being sentenced, Fox angrily shook his fist at the judge and loudly admonished him to 'quake in the face of God'. The phrase stuck so that Fox and his followers became known colloquially as 'Quakers'.

It is the ghost of this powerful, charismatic preacher that walks in Lower Brailes. He is seen striding past the meeting house of the Society of Friends as if off on one of his preaching tours that took him around Britain and as far afield as the West Indies and northern Germany.

The magnificent tower of Brailes church. The lanes close to the church are home to a sad phantom.

Fox may be the most famous ghost at Brailes, but he is far from being the only one. An anonymous man lurks on the bridge that carries the road to Shipston over a small stream. He is seen most often as dusk falls over the village, but although he is there fairly frequently there is nothing about him to indicate why he haunts the spot. The ghost merely stands quietly as if minding its own business.

More substantial is the ghostly young woman who lurks around the church and nearby lanes. This unfortunate girl became pregnant without taking the precaution of being married first and was heartlessly spurned by her child's father. The girl's family took the baby from her and sent it off to live with distant relatives, in the hope that a scandal could thereby by avoided. All they achieved was the utter misery of their daughter, who took sick and died.

The ghost wanders the lanes in obvious distress. Perhaps she is seeking her lost child, or maybe she curses the rogue who deserted her – we cannot tell.

LONG COMPTON

The strange old woman whose phantom appears at Long Compton is one of the numerous witches that local legends tell us have lived in Warwickshire and cast spells, both good and bad, on the local folk. This witch, however, is very much historic fact.

In 1879 Anne Tennant was found dead; clearly she had been murdered. It did not take the police long to identify the culprit as a farm labourer named James Hayward. The man had been muttering for some weeks that he was suffering from a curse put on him by Anne Tennant, well known locally as having skill with herbal remedies. She was, Hayward had declared on the morning of the killing, a witch and he was going to have things out with her.

The bare slopes of Harrow Hill north of Long Compton were the scene for a gruesome murder that led to a gentle haunting.

At his trial, Hayward was declared mad and sent to an asylum. But the ghost of Anne Tennant soon came to Long Compton, wearing her habitual black shawl and walking with a stooped back. She potters around the village, apparently aimlessly, popping up almost at random.

LITTLE COMPTON

A tragedy led to the haunting of Little Compton, one that left its indelible mark on this pretty little place. The parish church of St Denys was largely rebuilt in Victorian times, though a good deal remains of the medieval original, including the unusual hip-roofed tower. The church is dedicated to the patron saint of France due to the fact that from its founding in 1056 to 1467 it was owned by the Abbey of St Denys in Paris.

The church at Little Compton,
where a tangled love triangle led
to a tragedy in Victorian times.

In mid-Victorian times, the church had a choir famed for the excellence of its music. And the star of the choir was the beautiful young Miss Fielding. Inevitably she attracted the attentions of the local bachelors, including the curate, Mr Drane, and Captain Brandon who lived at The Grange. It was perhaps natural that Miss Fielding preferred the wealthy Captain Brandon to her other admirers and in due course they became engaged.

When it came time for the wedding, it fell to Curate Drane to conduct the service. He performed the marriage admirably, betraying no hint of the emotional turmoil within. At the end of the ceremony he claimed a kiss from the bride, refused an invitation to the wedding breakfast and waved the happy couple on their way. That evening the verger found Curate Drane hanging in the belfry.

The unhappy ghost of the curate has returned time and again to the churchyard. He is said to appear most often when weddings are taking place. Perhaps he longs for the matrimonial happiness that he was forbidden in life.

•Index•